"I've known Derek for two decades, heard him teach and preach, and have had many wonderful conversations with him. This book is a culmination of a life-time journey. It takes what could be an overwhelming subject and makes it personal and accessible to all. For a generation that wants it broken down and metaphorically digestible, this is the big picture in an album of great photos."

Frank Naea
*Former International President of Youth With A Mission*
*Auckland, New Zealand*

"An uncommonly wise planter of the Kingdom, Derek consistently and innovatively deliberates outside the lines. In this book, he teaches us to know our Creator and accept with gratitude who we've been made to be. Then, we're equipped and motivated to plant the living God into the hearts and minds of others."

La Prelle Martin, PhD
*Leadership and Program Development,*
*University of the Nations, Kona, Hawaii, USA*

"Derek skillfully relates captivating true stories, adeptly uses the Bible, and then suddenly connects it all to real-life issues that I'm going through right now. This is the kind of book you buy, read, recommend to friends and then read again."

Jeff Cheek
*Managing Director, Homes of Hope*
*Mexico*

"The genius of this book is in its ability to clarify the meaning of being a Christian: discover and engage with our loving God, then plant what we've learned into the lives of people around us. Derek helps us know God – so we know Whom we are planting – and then inspires our potting projects. This is the one book that church leaders and pastors will find empowered to equip their members!"

John K Choi
*Pastor of 2nd Gen. English Ministry*
*Open Worship, Tacoma Central Presbyterian Church ECO*
*Tacoma, Washington, USA*

# PLANTING GOD

## DEREK SCHOENHOFF

Sean,
May the love of God
be your anchor and
His power your shield.

Derek

# ACKNOWLEDGMENTS

So many people have contributed to the understandings of God I share in this book: my parents, who raised me in a godly family; my brother, who has such a sharp mind for truth; amazing professors in university and seminary who guided me in my learning; peers that I've worked with, who have been my *iron sharpening iron*; role models, like Loren Cunningham, whose obedience to God opened so many doors for people like me, or Ken Hemphill and Bob Reccord, on whose church staffs I was privileged to serve; members of my congregation in Hawaii, who have always been encouraging and supportive; and of course my amazing wife, who believes that my work is a valuable and important contribution to the world.

Thank you all - you're deeply loved.

# CONTENTS

*Forward*

When I first met Derek, he was speaking in Indianapolis, Indiana, and a group of us stayed up into the wee hours of the morning engrossed in deep discussion. As he shared with us, I learned that God speaks, that we can have intimate relationship with Him, and from that relationship, our lives can be radically transformed. At the time, I had no idea of how true that would become for me.

I took Derek's teaching and continued to try to connect with my Creator. Just the tiniest step towards a more intimate relationship with God and it felt like He swept in, scooped me up, and just held me so divinely and deliciously close. Over the coming months, God revealed himself. And there was light.

To my delight, I discovered that God was not elusive and distant. He was not like the kind, but uninterested, father figure of my childhood who provided only for my basic needs as any good father does. No. This father, my Heavenly Father, was very interested in me because He created me to reflect His glory. Strength built upon strength was what I found as I shed off my brokenness, shame and victim mentality. I exchanged it all for the most authentic relationship I could've ever imagined.

And He pursued me. God desired my love. Not a passive casual desire. He desired me in fierce and deliberate ways. And He wanted to bless me. Blessing upon blessing.

When I got my mind wrapped around the teaching Derek was delivering, my world – the world I have dominion over – split wide open in possibility.

He restored my health.

He redeemed my body.

He poured in beauty, peace, and joy.

He multiplied relationships.

My vocational calling became clear.

Resources poured in.

And I began to bear fruit.

I walked in a power I had never been aware of. I became the daughter of the King that I had always been. I stopped standing in the darkness and moved into light. I will never be the same.

This book delivers an understanding of God that will awaken something in your spirit. With an experienced dexterity that comes from teaching this material for almost two decades in close to a hundred nations, Derek is able to take difficult concepts and make them wonderfully easy to comprehend. He uses the Bible as his foundation and opens our eyes to its application in our everyday life with engaging true stories and vibrant insights. As you read *Planting God*, you'll feel hand-led through the nature and character of our heavenly Father in a way that empowers and inspires you.

I'm so glad Derek made the effort to plant what he's learned about God into my life, and now I'm thrilled he has done the same for all of you. When I come across an author that helps shape my understanding of God and encourages me in my faith, I have to tell people about their book. I'm sure you'll want to do the same!

Marcia Barnes

*Sells Group, President*

*Prologue*

In three out of the four New Testament gospels, the writers document Jesus telling the story of a farmer sowing seed on a variety of soils. When He told the story, Jesus was outside, by a lake, and there were so many people pressing in to hear what He was saying, that He decided to speak from a small boat.

"As the farmer was scattering the seed," Jesus said, His voice carrying over the din of the crowd, "Some fell along the path, and the birds came and ate it up. Some fell on rocky places, where it did not have much soil. It sprang up quickly, because the soil was shallow. But when the sun came up, the plants were scorched, and they withered because they had no root. Other seed fell among thorns, which grew up and choked the plants. Still other seed fell on good soil, where it produced a crop – a hundred, sixty or thirty times what was sown. Whoever has ears, let them hear." (Matthew 13:1-23)

Later, Jesus explained that the parable had to do with the "knowledge of the secrets of the kingdom of heaven." When people hear the message and do not understand it, He said, "the evil one comes and snatches away what was sown in their hearts." If someone hears the word and gladly receives it, but then their passion dies away – they are like the seed falling on rocky ground and their joy only lasts a short time. When pressure comes, they "quickly fall away." He said the seed falling on thorns refers to a person who hears the word, but the "worries of this life and the deceitfulness of wealth choke the word, making it unfruitful."

Further down in the chapter, in verse thirty-seven, Jesus says, "The one who sowed the good seed is the Son of Man."

Surely, nobody else can sow seed that is truly *good* – He is the only One.

About the seed that falls on good soil, Jesus said it refers to someone who "hears the word and understands it." This is good seed and this is good soil. And *these* people, our Lord affirms, produce "a crop, yielding a hundred, sixty or thirty times what was sown." How does that happen? How does seed produce a successful crop? The seed multiplies! New seed, from the exact DNA of the original seed, is re-sown.

Whether the soil was a hardened path, rocky ground, full of thorns, or a moist and fertile soil, all the soils had one thing in common: the good seed fell on them. As Jesus explained that process, people *heard*.

In the past few decades, there has been a lot of emphasis on *church planting*, *starting a ministry*, or *pioneering* a new Christian work. It is all contributing to an incredible growth of the Kingdom of God and is truly thrilling to witness. In the process, people are discovering that a church building should not be our goal, a new ministry with larger crowds should not be our goal, and new projects should not be our goal. Really, our goal shouldn't even be to plant a structure or a program, but to plant what we've learned of God directly into the lives of people around us and then discovering what it is that He would like to grow – it might not even look like a church or have a model for us to copy.

But if this is going to happen, we need a clear understanding of who God really is and how we can relate to Him. We need to carefully learn about His character and His personality. And we need to understand about ourselves and how marvelously we were made in His image. When we have this in our minds, we can thoughtfully and effectively be *Planting God*.

# 1 | Reversing the Great Commission

I'll always remember hurrying across campus to get to my first seminary class with the legendary Dr. Roy Fish, distinguished professor of Evangelism at Southwestern Baptist Theological Seminary in Fort Worth, Texas. It was a chilly morning that demanded a brisk pace and the dark clouds seemed to be ominously predicting light snow or heavy rain. I readjusted my backpack as I entered the large rotunda doors and made my way downstairs to his classroom, trying to shrug off the nervous energy that comes with starting something new. There was a vacant seat in the front row, on the far right side, and I quickly sat down, took a deep breath, and prepared to take notes. Dr. Fish entered the lecture room right on time and the pre-class chatter died down in eager anticipation of what this dearly loved and respected man of God would share with us.

"Good morning, everyone," he said into a little microphone that he always brought and hooked up to a small speaker on the table in front of him. A few people returned the greeting, while others just stared, as if even his greeting was something to never forget. Dr. Fish wrinkled his brow and solemnly declared, "Class, we have reversed the Great Commission." He pursed his lips and nodded solemnly. "By and large – we have inverted it."

I was stunned. "Have we really?" I wondered.

He was referring, of course, to the section in Matthew 28:19-20, where Jesus commands all of His disciples, "Therefore go and make disciples of all nations, baptizing them in the name of the Father and of the Son and of the Holy Spirit, and teaching them to obey everything I have commanded you. And surely I am with you always, to the very end of the age." Another passage like it is in Mark 16:15-16, when Jesus said, "Go into all the world and preach the gospel to all creation. Whoever believes and is baptized will be saved, but whoever does not believe will be condemned."

"The Great Commission," Dr. Fish continued, "says to go and tell." He paused, looking at each of us, "But we have said, come and listen."

The room was very quiet.

"So we have built bigger buildings, spent more money on style, lighting, sound systems, and relevant music. We establish more programs, desperately create greater shows and work tirelessly in an effort to get people to come to our thing. Listen. We don't need to get people to come to our thing – we need to go to where the people already are! Jesus did not say for us to pray that harvest would come to the workers, but that the Lord of the harvest would send workers to the harvest."

I quickly turned to Matthew 9:38 and Luke 10:2. Dr. Fish was right, of course; it's exactly what Jesus had said and the implications were huge.

When I had returned to my studio apartment, my mind was swirling with questions. *Were we in danger of some hideous side track? Were we, in fact, reversing Jesus' Great Commission?*

The only solution was to go back to the Bible and ask the Holy Spirit for guidance. As I thought about it, I needed to understand more about the Lord of the harvest and who He was. Then I needed to try and figure out how we could get back to going and telling. Over the years, it's become a passion of mine.

What I've realized since those early seminary days, is that there can be many misconceptions in our minds about God. I've recognized that our deceptive enemy, spoken of by Jesus in John 8, doesn't seem to care if we embrace a specific aspect of God's character, as long as that's all we embrace. If all we believe in is the grace of God, for example, then we are unable to Biblically explain His judgment and wrath. This can lead to a casual dismissal of the reality of sin and its effects on our lives, families and communities; it can cause us to speak of hell as if it didn't exist; it can cause people to think that God will overlook shameful behavior.

On the other hand, if all we see is God's judgment and wrath, it can lead to lives occupied with criticism, gossip and judgment; we can easily be trapped into living lives full of bitterness, resentment and unforgiveness; and people can think that God is full of rage and constantly disappointed with almost all of our life choices.

A good friend of mine called this latter result, "living in a shame zone." He goes on to describe a person who was a brilliant piano player.

One day, when this musician was younger, his mother came home and demanded, "Did you practice your piano?"

"Yes," he answered, truthfully.

His mother's eyes narrowed disapprovingly, "Well, your room's a mess!"

This young pianist described to my friend how it seemed like nothing he ever did could meet the expectations of his parents. Every time he would try to meet them, they would just raise their demands and he would live his younger years in this shame zone. Since his parents were the supreme authority figures in his life as a child, when he met God – the supreme authority figure for us all – and became a Christian, he transferred that feeling of shame into his new relationship with his Savior. He viewed our heavenly Father as someone who was never really happy with him, as someone whose expectations he always fell short of, and as someone who viewed him as the great disappointment.

These warped perspectives of God can impact us deeply and truly influence our life decisions and how we treat people. They can skew our perception of how God sees us and even decimate how we see ourselves. Not only do these distorted ideas impact us as individuals, but we can extend them into the community around us with devastating effects. To continue with our example, entire churches can sway into a theology of grace, for instance, that doesn't line up with the Word of God – or they can swing to a theology of judgment and wrath that leaves grace alone on the side of the street.

I don't think it's possible for us to have a perfect perception of God. Paul writes in I Corinthians 13:12 that we only see a dim reflection, as in a mirror. But, despite the dimness, God has perfectly revealed Himself to us because everything He does is perfect. In his letter to the Romans,

Paul explains that God has made Himself so plain to us and easy to understand, that people will be without excuse in their knowledge of God. In Romans 1:20, he wrote, "For since the creation of the world God's invisible qualities – His eternal power and divine nature – have been clearly seen, being understood from what has been made, so that people are without excuse." So even though we have an imperfect view of God because His revelation is not yet complete, He has perfectly revealed all we need to know of Him. As a matter of fact, God has revealed so much of Himself to us that we are without excuse. Paul continued to write that one day, we would see God fully when we're face to face. At that time, our revelation of Him will be perfectly complete.

I guess what I'm most excited about in my relationship with God, is knowing that I've never fully arrived, but I'm always on this exciting journey of discovering more and more about God. We should not be content with what we have already learned, but we should be passionately hungry to discover more of Him and His love for us.

It's like a guy and a girl who are initially attracted to each other. At first, they know a little bit about each other, but something in them wants to know more. There is a desire in them to spend more time together and invest in a relationship. Why? Because they want to get to know the other person and they want the other person to get to know them. In Jeremiah 24:7, we see God transferring this idea to the prophet when He said of the Israelites, "I will give them a heart to know me, that I am the Lord. They will be my people, and I will be their God, for they will return to me with all their heart."

God revealed himself perfectly, although incompletely, and gave us a desire to know Him more. That wonderful process happens in the safety of the covenant relationship He has made with us and when we discover the depth of His love, our lives are forever changed.

Don't we love witnessing that desire for Jesus and the ensuing transformation? Nothing is more exciting than meeting brilliant young people who are thirsting after God. Weary of the disintegrating opinions around them, they are passionately desiring to know and apply Truth to their lives. Whether they be part of the more than 600 million people under the age of twenty-five in India; the vast amount of Koreans who are disillusioned with legalistic systems of religion, but hungry for vibrant relationship with God; a growing core of young Americans who still believe in a right and a wrong; young Europeans who are starting to understand that the foundations of their nations are important to preserve and defend; Latinos who are channeling their passions into missions; or youthful Africans who are rising up with courage, humility, and determination – knowing deep in their hearts that the time for them to shine is now; there is a sweeping global desire among many people to be light in a dark world instead of being a candle with no wick.

Solomon wrote in Ecclesiastes 12:1, "Remember your Creator in the days of your youth, before the days of trouble come and the years approach when you will say, 'I find no pleasure in them' ..."

Speaking of our Creator, let's take a closer look at how He has revealed Himself to us through the book that He wrote. It's a great one! As we look at it more closely, I think we'll learn a lot about Him, together.

## 2 | Discovering Our Creator and His Character

One of the greatest challenges any author faces is how to begin their book. They want to capture readers, set the tone, and inspire people to keep reading. I don't think it was any different for God when He thought about what to write and how to start His book; He picked a brilliant launching point.

In Genesis 1:1 we read, "In the beginning ..."

What a masterful way to start this life-changing book we call the *Bible*. Already we have some very serious and foundational questions answered for us. There was a beginning! And apparently, someone who knows something about it is going to tell us what happened.

The next word tells us more when we read, "In the beginning, God ..."

I can imagine the thought our Creator put into His opening line. He was probably pondering how, in one phrase, He could answer our questions. *How did life start? How did we get onto this planet we call earth? Is there anyone who really has these answers? Can we really know? Do we have some kind of purpose to our lives?* With one line, one simple statement, so many of our questions find an answer. There at the beginning, witnessing the birth of the earth and humanity itself, was God.

He continues to share about Himself with the very next word. "In the beginning, God created." With a sigh of relief, humanity finds its Designer! God's first title, other than God, is *Creator.* He is the Master Artist, the One who invents, the Instigator of life, the Architect of universal physics, science, art, business, economics and poetry. He is the Thoughtful Planner.

What did He create?

"In the beginning, God created the heavens and the earth." He created everything we know. He created things we see and things we have yet to discover. As it turns out, this world was not a random accident of crashing neutrons; rather, it was the purposeful design of Divine neurons.

The marvelous thing about our Creator is that He has never stopped creating. We read in 2 Corinthians 5:17, "Therefore, if anyone is in Christ, the new creation has come: The old has gone, the new is here!" So one of the things God is still creating is a new *you!* A work in progress perhaps, but if those who are in Christ are a *new creation,* someone must be doing the creating. It could only be the work of our original Designer, our Creator God.

Verse three is uniquely exciting. Not only did God create, but He *reveals Himself to us.* In most English versions it reads something like, "And God said, 'Let there be light,' and there was light." Interestingly, that light wasn't the stars, the moon or the sun. Those weren't created until verse fourteen. So what *light* became visible?

In John 1:3,4 we read, "Through Him all things were made; without Him nothing was made that has been made. In

Him was life, and that life was the *light* of men." In Revelation 21:23, when John was writing about the new city he saw in the heavenlies, he penned, "The city does not need the sun or the moon to shine on it, for the glory of God gives it *light* ..." The prophet Isaiah wrote, "The people walking in darkness have seen a great *light*; on those living in the land of deep darkness a *light* has dawned." (Isaiah 9:2) Could it be that the *light* in Genesis 1 is actually God revealing *Himself* to us? Yes!

This is important, because right there, in the beginning of the Bible, we already learn one of the great things about God: He longs for His creation to know Him. He is not some mysterious God we cannot know or understand – as a matter of fact, He says just the opposite. In Jeremiah 33:3, we read about God saying, "Call to me and I will answer you and tell you great and mysterious things you do not know." God actually looks forward to revealing Himself to us – even His more mysterious aspects. He is the light in the darkness of our lives, He sheds light on the issues of life, and His Word lights up the path in front of us.

I remember meeting a young woman who was a fashion designer in New York. Somehow we got onto the topic of whether or not God speaks to us. She wasn't a Christian and was very skeptical about the whole idea. So we moved on to talk about something else. She told me about her recent job change and talked about how she had worked for a small but very successful company, and was one of their favored artists, but had been unhappy. A few months before we met, she had just switched fashion companies and was much happier where she was.

"What was the difference?" I asked her.

"I really wasn't comfortable at my old company. The CEO and top executives would party constantly, spend tons of company money on prostitutes and drugs, and were totally disconnected from the rest of us."

"You didn't like that?"

"I felt like my talents and my contributions as a designer were just being wasted on their lavish parties. I almost felt prostituted myself! It was as if they were just using me and then wasting the money that came from my hard work. I actually felt like I was financing their parties with my designs."

It made sense. "What made you leave?" I asked her.

"I had a thought. 'This is not right. I'm paying for these parties with my sweat, tears and passion. It is a waste of my artistic talent.' So I decided to quit. I looked for a different company and found this one." She pointed to the building behind her.

"Things are better now?"

"Much better. This company is owned by Christians – not that it matters, I guess – but they actually have company-wide profit-sharing. I feel respected, encouraged and safe – I think all the employees feel that way. And trust me, in the world of fashion – this place is a very rare find."

I thought for a few moments and remembered James 1:17. It reads, "Every good thing given and every perfect gift is from above, coming down from the Father of lights, with whom there is no variation or shifting shadow." (NASB)

I turned to her and asked, "You know the thought you had? The one where you thought, *This is not right?*"

"Yeah?"

"That was a *good* thought."

She nodded.

"Did you know that it was God speaking to you?"

She raised her eyebrows.

"The Bible tells us that *everything good* – comes from Him. So the thought that nudged you – the thought that said to you *this isn't right* was actually Him speaking to you. He wanted to get you out of there – to rescue you – and because He is our light, He was actually lighting up a pathway out of the darkness to a better place. That's the kind of God He is. You can see how much He cares about you."

She asked me several more questions about God and how He interacts with us. Before the day ended, she had asked Jesus to come into her heart and life, to "rescue her from herself." She repented of her past sin, and even forgave people who had hurt her.

God is a God who loves to be seen. Jesus says in John 12:45, "The one who looks at me is seeing the one who sent me." And God invites us to know Him. We read in Ephesians 1:17, "I keep asking that the God of our Lord Jesus Christ, the glorious Father, may give you the Spirit of wisdom and revelation, so that you may know him better." He even encourages us to call to Him, to seek Him with all of our hearts, and to delight in Him (Jeremiah 33:3; Jeremiah 29:10; Psalm 37:4 and 23).

God was there at the beginning, He is our Creator, and He reveals Himself as light to us. How amazing is that? By choosing to show us Himself as light, He is encouraging us out of darkness and into the safety of His bright healing presence. After all, I've never heard of anyone afraid of the light, have you? I've met plenty of people who were afraid of the dark though. John writes in 1 John 1:5, "God is light; in Him there is no darkness at all."

There is this wonderful passage in Exodus where Moses asks God a surprising question. Moses had witnessed God do tremendously powerful acts. He had seen God afflict the

Egyptians with plagues, he had seen God turn water into blood, a stick into a snake, and the dramatic parting of the Red Sea so that the Israelites would have a pathway out of Egypt. He knew God had drowned Pharaoh and his army as they tried to pursue and reclaim their escaped slaves, he'd seen Him provide mana and quail when the people were hungry, and he had heard God speak to him "as one speaks to a friend." (Exodus 33:11) All of that is recorded in the book of Exodus. Yet, in the midst of those demonstrations of power, there was still a throbbing question in the heart of Moses – and maybe it is a question in our hearts, too, as we cry out, "But who are You? What are You like?" Moses cried out to the Almighty, "God show me your glory!" (Exodus 33:18). He was implying, "God, I want to know *who* You are, not just witness Your power demonstrations."

God responded, as He promises us He will if we cry out to Him. He agrees to meet Moses on Mount Sinai. As the Lord passes in front of the Israelite leader, He declares that He is, "The Lord, the Lord, the compassionate and gracious God, slow to anger, abounding in love and faithfulness, maintaining love to thousands, and forgiving wickedness, rebellion and sin. Yet he does not leave the guilty unpunished; he punishes the children and their children for the sin of the fathers to the third and fourth generation."

What a staggering revelation! He tells Moses that He is *compassionate* and *gracious*. I don't know about you, but I get excited with just those two aspects of His character. Compassionate means that God feels for us and acts on our behalf. It is more than just empathy or pity – it includes action. We see a great example of this in Exodus 3:6,7, when God says, "I have indeed seen the misery of my people in Egypt. I have heard them crying out because of their slave drivers, and I am concerned about their suffering. So I have *come down to rescue them* from the hand of the Egyptians ..." He didn't just see, He wasn't just concerned, but He was compelled to action *because* of what was happening to His people.

There are many who see the suffering of humanity, but do little to help. Have you ever wondered why we see celebrities posing with poor people in Africa? Why don't they pose with the people in the poorest neighborhood right next to where they live? It's probably because it would expose their hypocrisy. They care less for the poor and more about creating an image that will enhance and promote their own wealth and success.

God not only sees the suffering, He says, "I'm going to come down and rescue them." That's compassion.

*Gracious* means He acts with kindness towards those who love Him – there is poise and protocol in how God interacts with His children. He doesn't yell at us like an outraged boss. He gently leads us through pathways of restoration and hope. There is no crisis that throws God into a panic; He is steadfast and sure (Hebrews 6:19, NASB).

The next statement is just as amazing. God says to Moses that He is *slow to anger*. Those three words make a deep impression on people. In our society today, people seem to fly into a rage over the smallest things. Is it really possible to be slow to anger? We have lots to learn from God if we are truly made in His image.

Then, God speaks of His *abounding love* and *faithfulness*. In other words, there is an endless supply of God's love. Notice, too, that He groups love with faithfulness. True love is a love that remains faithful. Regardless of life's challenges, good or bad times, confusions or disillusionments, what enables us to not only survive, but overcome, is faithful love. The faithful love of God provides the foundation for all wedding vows spoken between a husband and a wife in nations around the world as they say, "I will never leave you or forsake you." Sadly, although it is an underpinning for us, we can sometimes speak these things and then proceed to disrupt them. God, however, makes a covenant of faithfulness to His people that He never breaks; He is always faithful. Deuteronomy 32:4 reads, "He is the Rock, His works are perfect, and all His ways are just. A faithful God who does no wrong, upright and just is He."

Not only is He abounding in love, but I like the way God tells Moses that He *maintains love*.

For many years I lived on the beautiful island of Hawaii – in the Hawaiian chain of islands – and I often got asked to officiate at weddings. I loved to do it. Something I liked to remind couples of, was that, "Love takes maintenance." It's like a car. If you don't put oil in it, the head gasket will explode. If you don't put gas in it, it won't start. If you just leave it in a field – over time it will be rusted out and destroyed. So it is with any relationship – especially the relationship between husband and wife. If you have ever been in a relationship of both giving love and receiving love, you know this is true. If we don't take the time, energy or resources to maintain love, the relationship deteriorates. It may eventually fall apart. I encouraged the couples to have a maintenance program for their relationship – from going on dates and doing fun things together, to attending marriage conferences as a couple or strategizing for how they can help other people in need, together. Relationships really do need maintenance.

Isn't it wonderful to hear God tell Moses that He *maintains* love? He does so much to keep our relationship with Him fresh and vibrant. We'll learn more about that in this book.

Of course, the only way this kind of love is possible, the only way this kind of grace is available, and the only way we are able to interact with God in this way, is because of the ability to forgive and be forgiven. God tells Moses that He *forgives wickedness, rebellion and sin.*

Forgiveness is simply, but not always easily, choosing to *not* hold someone's sin against them. It is saying, "Although you grieved me and caused such pain and hurt, I will no longer hold it against you." Of course, God is the one who gives us this definition. In 2 Corinthians 5:18-19, He states, "All this is from God, who reconciled us to Himself through Christ and gave us the ministry of reconciliation: that God was reconciling the world to Himself in Christ, not counting people's sins against them."

Finally, He tells Moses that He has his back. He reassures Moses that the *guilty will be punished.* It is not something we have a responsibility for, unless we are in a position of authority or a judge, but we can know that God will be the steward of justice issues. He relieves us of the need for retaliation and revenge. What a burden that would be, if it was ours to avenge! And what fear we would live in … knowing that others were out to avenge themselves on us. How awesome of God to take this upon Himself – with His wisdom, His understanding and His power.

After the revelation of God's character, His glory, to Moses – for the first time in the recorded history of that great leader, we read that he responds by falling flat on his face before God and worshipping Him. What an intimate, holy moment ... worshipping our Creator.

I've heard people say that the God of the Old Testament seems so different from the God in the New Testament. And while I understand what they are saying, I'm not so sure they are correct. We've just looked at an Old Testament passage where God openly shows us that He is compassionate, gracious, slow to anger, abounding in love and faithfulness, maintaining love, forgiving, and punishing the guilty. One the other hand, I do think that the story of the Old Testament – one before the work of Christ – shows us what we really deserve and probably would have gotten, had God not intervened with the grace of Jesus. This doesn't mean our actions will not have consequences – the wages of sin is still death, but Jesus provides our pathway to freedom.

As an aside, if someone has not had a good example of a father in their life, I point them to this passage in Exodus as well. Really, the revelation of God to Moses is the revelation of His character as Father. A godly father needs only to look at this list, look at his own life and ask the questions, "Am I slow to anger? Am I abounding in love and faithfulness? Am I compassionate and gracious?" As we work on being more like God, we are able to display His glory to others and He is able to be glorified through us. The glory of God, as it turns out, is not some nebulous concept. We can check, "Is the character of God visible in my character too?" That's what it means to glorify God in our lives. Of course that isn't just for fathers, but for all of us who call ourselves Christians.

So – to start His book, God tells us there was a beginning, He was present at the beginning, He actually *is* the Artist behind the art – the Creator, and He reveals Himself to us as Light. What a great start! Then He gives us an even more intimate portrait of His character as we eavesdrop in on His conversation with Moses in Exodus 34. This is certainly wonderful information we can plant into the lives of people around us.

But how can we be sure God is truly God? And what makes a being "God" anyway? Was Krishna such a being? Was Buddha? What makes the Creator God of the Bible, the real *God*? Are there some specific qualities someone needs to possess in order to be qualified as not just a *god*, but *God*?

# 3 | Clearly Seeing His Invisible Qualities

The first chapter of the book of Romans is quite the start to a letter. Probably none of us have ever received a letter about God from any of our friends that is so impressive, so important and so well written. (I often wonder if the art of letter writing is completely dead in our day of hurriedly-written text messages and pithy heat-of-the-moment social media opinions.)

In this opening chapter of his letter to the Christians in Rome, Paul presents answers to the questions we have posed about God.

We read in Romans 1:18-20:

> The wrath of God is being revealed from heaven against all the godlessness and wickedness of people, who suppress the truth by their wickedness, since what may be known about God is plain to them, because God has made it plain to them. For since the creation of the world God's invisible qualities—His eternal

power and divine nature—have been clearly seen, being understood from what has been made, so that people are without excuse.

What a remarkable passage! Don't fixate on the word "wrath" at the moment. Some people get all amped up about the wrath of God only to miss out on some of the profundity here. There is certainly a place for us to talk about judgment and wrath, particularly God's, but Paul is not writing about the wrath of God as much as he is writing about what *sparked* God's wrath. It shouldn't surprise us that the wrath of God in Romans 1 is similar to the wrath of God in Genesis 6 – with the story of Noah and the flood. We can only assume that the broken heart of God we read about in Genesis 6:6 would apply here as well.

Paul is telling the Christians grouping in Rome that God made Himself plain and understandable to us – so easy to know, in fact, that people are "without excuse." They have *no* excuse. We cannot say, "I'm sorry, God, I searched for you and just couldn't find you. You were too hidden. Too complicated. Too mysterious. Too confusing." We read that God has made Himself plain since the "creation of the world" – since the very beginning.

The natural question is, "How did God make things about Himself plain to us?" Paul fills us in on the logic. He writes in verse twenty, "For since the creation of the world, God's invisible qualities – His eternal power and divine nature – have been clearly seen, being understood from what has been made."

Did you know God is invisible to us, but He's not invisible? John 4:24 says, "God is spirit, and His worshippers must worship in spirit and in truth." So God is not visible to us because He is Spirit but that doesn't mean He is invisible. We read that Stephen, right before he was stoned to death – the account in Acts 7, "… looked up to heaven and saw the glory of God, and Jesus standing at the right hand of God." He saw the glory of God; Jesus; and God, the Father. In Isaiah 6:1, the prophet writes, "In the year that King Uzziah died, I saw the Lord, high and exalted, seated on a throne; and the train of His robe filled the temple."

So, God is not invisible, but Paul writes that He has *invisible qualities* – much like all of us. When we meet someone for the first time, we see their visible qualities. We make note of their hair color, their eye color, their height, their smile, and their physique, but their invisible qualities take more effort to discover. Are they a kind person? What do they value? Are they shy or outgoing? Do they have a sense of humor? What are their goals and dreams? These are all qualities that are invisible at first, but eventually, we get to know them if we stay interested long enough.

Just because God is Spirit and invisible to us, does not mean He is not knowable. Do you notice a little play on words as Paul writes God's qualities are "invisible", but He can be "clearly seen?" Even so, there is a deeper point Paul is making. God is so desiring for us to know who He is, that He has made even His invisible qualities – His innermost personality – visible.

The apostle goes on to define exactly what God's invisible qualities are: His "eternal power" and "divine nature." How is it possible to know the invisible qualities of God? Well, Paul wrote that we can understand them from "what has been made." Creation itself displays the Creator. We can know about the Artist by carefully studying His art.

The first invisible quality of God visible in His creation, is God's "eternal power." This means that God is *unlimited* in His ability to create new things and to restore. God can create new life, new structures, new ministries, and new ways of doing things. His ideas are most often shared with us in the place of prayer. He is also fully capable of bringing restoration and healing into our lives by the unrestricted power of the blood of Jesus and through the counsel of the Holy Spirit.

In Mark 3:5, there is a story of a man whose hand was withered. Jesus called out to him in front of the people and asked him to stretch out his withered hand. As he did, Mark recounts that his hand was "completely restored." God has the power to completely restore. As a matter of fact, I believe that the entire ministry of Jesus can be summed up in one word: restoration.

"Divine nature" refers to being organized and detailed in His *emperorship*, for lack of a better term. Here, the word *divine* is not a mystical word, quite the opposite. It speaks of God's organization, planning and love for detail. Anyone who looks at the wonder of what God has produced can tell that the Artist is very organized and structured, yet creative, surprising, and awe-inspiring. Paul writes we can know these aspects of God by looking at what has been made – the creation produced by our Creator. There are literally millions of things that point to God's power to create and His ability to structure things perfectly, but let's just look at a few specific examples.

If we examine animals, for instance, it doesn't take long for a pattern to emerge. Wolves travel in packs. Whales are in pods. Fish are in schools. Sheep are in flocks. Flies are in hoards. Geese are in gaggles. Elk live in gangs. Lions are in prides. Apes hang around in troops. Buffalo roam in herds. Horses thunder in a harass. Jays are said to be a party. The list goes on and on. What does this tell us about God? He's the one who said, in Genesis 2:18, "It is not good for man to be alone." He did not create us to be independent or uncommitted to a group, but rather God made us to be committed to each other and interdependent. There's even one specific gaggle of geese, known as Canada Geese, which fly in V formations. One of these geese, after flying by itself for sixty miles, will collapse in exhaustion. But if that same goose were to fly in the V, rotating the leader every thirty miles and drifting in the slipstream of the goose ahead, it can travel more than 2500 miles in one flight. Isn't that amazing? I believe that not only are we to work with one another, but that God wants to work with us. It is truly not good for a person to be alone.

As we continue our observations of what has been made by God, we can notice seasons. What an important lesson this is! The bright green leaves display the freshness of spring. The warmth of summer brings us outdoors. The changing leaves of fall signal the coming of winter, a season of cold and snow. These changing seasons should encourage us to understand our lives, too. Everything goes in seasons. Our relationships with people go through seasons and even our relationship with God goes through seasons. We can know that after every winter, there is a spring coming. And that's what God promised in Genesis 8:22 "As long as the earth endures, seedtime and harvest, cold and heat, summer and winter, day and night will never cease."

In my relationship with God, I have sometimes felt dry and distant from Him or struggled to hear His voice and understand His leading. But seeing God's design of seasons,

I'm visibly reminded not to get discouraged. I know that if it were always "harvest season", I would be exhausted. The winter season is historically known as a season of rest, restoration and preparation for a new year when there's the coming of fresh things – the emergence of Spring.

One day I was looking at the magnificent scenery visible from the *lanai* of our home in Hawaii. The bright blue sky was inviting and spacious. The sunlight sparkled off the clear ocean water and a light breeze swept across my face. Suddenly, a thought popped into my head in the form of a question, "Derek, do you think the same Person who created all of this, immaculate in its aesthetics and perfect in its functions, could also manage the details of your life?" What a thought! Of course He can. The only thing blocking God from doing it, is when I get in the way.

Whether it be a beautifully choreographed sunset, perfect in timing and colors; the tiniest molecular structures interacting with each other, exact in their ebb and flow; or the grandeur of the star-filled galaxies, stunning and irresistibly interesting; nature offers us endless learning about who God is and how He works.

What becomes obvious, as we pursue studying His art, is that no other being or god is like our loving Creator. He is unlimited in His power and immaculate in His character. The work of His hands is flawless in its synchronization and design. He is the Emperor of emperors, the Leader of leaders, the only good Shepherd – He is God.

# 4 | He is Present, Active and Working

When we want to get to know a person, one of the most effective ways to further the relationship is to ask questions. It is both a basic way of introduction, as when we ask "What is your name?" for example, as well as a more intimate way of getting to know someone if we probe with deeper questions.

Our greatest example in the area of relationships, of course, is Jesus. God Himself, the Creator, became the created. Who better to learn about *how to be a human*, than from the One who created humans? What did He teach us when He walked the earth? Did He look down on those He came to save? How did Jesus interact with people?

Certainly, when the Lamb of God arrived on earth, He saw so much that was out of order. He saw people who hated each other when He knew they had been designed to love one another. He saw men treating women in ways that broke His designer heart. He saw parents who were quick to anger when parenting children. He saw children living in rebellion.

He saw institutions of government who abused their authority and legal systems by creating endless laws that burdened the people. Yet, He didn't start railing at everyone. As a matter of fact, Jesus' *modus operandi* was very different. He primarily employed story-telling and asking questions.

Isn't He a great model for us? I'm sure almost all of us have seen firsthand how we as Christians can be so susceptible to arrogance. After all, we know stuff about God and we have been commanded to share it with those who don't. We have something they need – in fact, it is something they are desperate to know. This can easily give us a superior attitude. Not so with Jesus; He walked in humility.

It might be a surprise for people to know that Jesus asked over three hundred recorded questions in the gospels. About a third of those questions were binary questions, but the majority of them were complex questions.

Binary questions only require two possible answers – like *yes* and *no*, for example. During the Last Supper, recorded in Luke 22, Jesus asked His disciples a binary question. We read in verse thirty-five, "Then Jesus asked them, 'When I sent you without purse, bag, or sandals, did you lack anything?'" Of course, the disciples answered *no*.

Complex questions, however, invite discussion and debate. Sometimes, Jesus asked His disciples what they were thinking, like in Matthew 17:25. In a discussion about kings and taxes, He asked Peter, "What do you think, Simon?" Another time He enquired, "What is the kingdom of God like? What shall I compare it to?" in Luke 13:18. These kinds of questions not only opened up opportunity for dialogue, but also established an atmosphere in which it was okay to ask questions.

Now, there are a few people who say we should not ask God *why* questions. Instead, we should ask, "God, what are you wanting to teach me?" This is incorrect for two reasons.

First, God does not always want to teach us. I realized this more when my wife and I had children. I don't always want to be a stream of information for my kids, constantly teaching them. Can you visualize that? My children would run away as I approached, knowing that I was about to dump hours of information on them. Most times, I just want to enjoy time with my kids – watching them play. I love laughing with them and I feel honored when they choose to cry on my shoulder. Many wonderful moments are when they just sit on my lap – leaning their heads against my chest – and resting. Indubitably, there are occasions when I teach them, but there are many more stretches when I revel in just being around them and playing with them.

Of course the questions come. I'm not threatened when they ask me *why* things happen. I tell them the answers they are ready to understand, if I know what they are. Sometimes, I don't know the answer, yet they persist in trying to find it! I marvel at them when they figure out something new.

Second, it's okay to ask God *why* because Jesus also asked *why* questions. If we really believe Jesus modeled how to live as a human, how to interact with the Father, and how to relate to each other, then asking *why* must be okay. Roughly twenty-five percent of the complex questions Jesus asked began with the word *why*. The deepest *why* question ever asked in the history of humanity, was when Jesus experienced the separation sin causes between us and God. He was hanging on the cross, having taken on the sins of the world, and as He felt the terror of His separation from the

Father, He cried out in a loud voice: "My God, My God, why have You forsaken Me?" (Matthew 27:46; Mark 15:34)

We can be free to ask God the tough questions, including the *why* questions. However, we must remember that God knows when we are able to bear the answer. My own son asked me a *why* question when he was four years old. He looked up at the sky and asked, "Dad, why is the sky blue?" I pondered the question and determined he was not ready to hear about *Rayleigh Scattering*. He wouldn't have understood that as light moves through the atmosphere, most of the longer wavelengths pass straight through the red, orange and yellow light largely affected by the air. His young mind wouldn't have processed the idea that the shorter wavelength light is absorbed by gas molecules and then the absorbed blue light radiates in different directions, getting scattered all around the sky. Because of that, whichever direction we look, this scattered blue light reaches us.

I came up with a simpler answer. "I guess it's because God thought blue was a great color for the sky. What do you think?"

He thought for a moment – running through various other colors in his mind. Then he looked at me and answered, "I think it is too, Dad."

In the same way, when we ask God *why* things have happened to us, we have to rest in knowing and trusting that God will share with us the answers when we are mature enough to hear them. We can ask our question, knowing the answer will come someday. Personally, I've found that He answers our questions when the timing is right.

Again, when he was four years old, my son came to me with the keys to a truck we had borrowed. I knew what was coming.

"Dad. Look what I have." The proud and expectant expression on his face was priceless.

I answered, "The keys to the truck."

"Yup." He stood there for a few moments waiting for me to make him an offer – but when none came, he decided to get right to the point. "Dad ... can I drive it?"

At this point, let me interject with a thought. We can ask God whatever we want. We can ask Him for understanding, for provision, for protection, for guidance, for healing, for creativity, and for how to do things – just to name a few – but at the end of the day, His wisdom is far superior to ours. What we need to determine in our hearts before we ask, is, "Are we ready and willing to accept His answer?"

I looked at my son and shook my head.

Of course his next question was, "Why not, Dad?"

At this point there is unbelief in his face. How could I be so mean as to not let him drive? Did I not see that he had the keys in his hand? Doesn't *having the keys* mean that he knows everything there is to know about driving a 1993 Toyota pickup with absolutely no power steering and a challenging stick shift?

He continued with deep disappointment in his voice, fighting back tears, and looking down at the ground. Then, with a twinge of hope, despite my firmness, he asks again, adding the word *please* and looking as humble as possible. He points out that he knows exactly where the keys go.

I explain to him – in simple terms – that he has to be sixteen years old. "It isn't my law, but it is the law imposed by the state of Hawaii."

He is not consoled. Now there's anger in his face. Other than going to the moon in a red rocket ship, the obvious next best thing would be to drive this truck. The anger is multidirectional at this point. It could go towards weeping with great sadness, exploding in frustration and throwing the keys on the ground, or just walking away in silent protest.

I sweep him into my arms. "Son, you are going to be a fantastic driver someday. I know you will have your own truck to drive. So, when you're old enough, I'll teach you how to drive your truck through the mud, over rocks, on the sand and all over this island. I'm sorry that you can't do it now, but let me show you some things about trucks that make them very cool, okay?"

He is ever so slightly encouraged. "Okay, Dad. I want my truck to be bright yellow with big red tires."

"That would be awesome!"

Soon we were laughing and playing again and the *you can't drive the truck* experience is momentarily behind us. He might try again later, but for now at least, all is well.

That's how it is with God. We're not always the most patient and humble children. He has to treat us with great love and patience.

Eventually, my son recovers. My hope is that the yes-you-can moments between him and me far outweigh the no-you-can't moments. I hope that he has confidence in his father and believes that I know what I'm doing. Maybe, at this stage, he doesn't realize there are things beyond his or my control. But later, he will see that I was calculating conditions, adhering to laws, leaning on wisdom I'd learned from life and doing it all with his best interests in mind.

Jesus asked amazing questions. He modeled the art of question asking for us. He asked Peter, "Who do you say that I am?" (Matthew 16:13-20) What a great question for disciples to contemplate! Do we say Jesus is our friend, King, and Savior? Or do we only see Him in His historical context?

Some people might say He's a liar and a fraud. Others might say He is someone with whom they have no relationship. Do they wish they knew Him more? Is Jesus just a picture on a wall, carrying a lamb, or is He their Master on an intimately personal level?

In Matthew 15:1-20, Jesus was asked by the Pharisees and teachers of the law, "Why do your disciples break the tradition of the elders?" That same question gets asked in many churches around the world today. We can love our traditions! Jesus responded with an insightful question, "Why do you break the command of God for the sake of your tradition?"

Ouch! Some of our traditions in the Body of Christ are wonderful; others might be breaking the commands of God.

After the interaction in that passage, the disciples came to Jesus and asked Him, "Do you know that the Pharisees were offended when they heard this?"

Today, there are many who would respond the same way to questions regarding their traditions – whether they be cultural or religious. They would get offended.

I have to interject here. I have never seen a time and age where people are so quick to be offended than during these modern days. It seems every time I turn around, I'm hearing or reading about a person who was offended by something, even things completely unrelated to them personally. I truly believe there is no offense that cannot be worked out at the foot of the cross. If we are constantly going to people with how they have offended us, or to courtrooms with how a group of people has offended us, or to the media because some religious symbol offended us – I believe we have forgotten something. *All of us have offended God terribly.* After that, we really have no right to take up offense. Instead, whatever offends us should be expressed to God and left at the foot of the cross. Then, we can resume our path with the same freedom and grace that is extended to us by Jesus. Even in the instance of taking up something that we know also offends God, if we do not lay it at His feet first, unhealthy rage and desires for vengeance will plant poisonous bitter roots into our lives. Whenever I meet a person who is easily offended, I know they have spent very little time at the foot of the cross.

Jesus posed another great question to a blind beggar, asking, "What would you like me to do for you?" (Luke 18:35-42). Why would He ask that? I remember hearing from counselors, therapists and psychologists that one of the first steps out of bondage is to admit your need. Jesus was getting this beggar to speak it out – to express his need – to say, "I am not happy like this. I don't enjoy being treated like this. I need you!" Of course, when Jesus healed him, he immediately received his sight and followed Christ – praising God, as it says in Luke's account.

There is a conversation in John 18 in which Jesus gets grilled by the high priest. He is falsely accused and at one point, slapped in the face by a nearby official. Can you imagine? After he'd endured all that, Jesus asks another poignant question, "If I said something wrong, testify as to what is wrong. But if I spoke the truth, why did you strike me?" This question is similar to another great question He asked in John 8, "If I am telling the truth, why don't you believe me?" So many people say they believe in God and even believe in Jesus, yet their lives do not reflect the carrying out of His commands. If these people were honest, the reality would be that they, in fact, do not believe in Jesus.

As I have reflected on the brilliant, timely, and effective questions that Jesus asked, I've realized my need for thoughtfully asking God some questions. The psalmist-king, David, writes in Psalm 17:6, "I call on you, O God, for you will answer me; give ear to me and hear my prayer."

There have been significant times in my life when I have asked difficult questions.

One time I asked God, "Why did You choose the method of the cross as Your vehicle of death?" It was a seminary question we had to deliberate while studying Systematic Theology, but I felt I hadn't quite grasped the answer. The question understands the sovereignty of God and mulls over why, when God can choose His poison, did the Father choose *the cross* for His Son. I would think that an easier way to die would have been by a heart attack, a pill, lethal injection or freezing to death. As a matter of fact, why didn't Jesus come during our modern age? Maybe His death would have been much more humane. Arriving on earth during the time of the Roman practice of crucifixion meant dying in a gruesome, public, humiliating, and horribly painful execution. He was paraded through the streets and demeaned with a crown of thorns that ripped through His scalp and was imbedding into His skull. He was whipped and tortured with ruthless repeated physical abuse. He was verbally abused, again and again. He was betrayed by a dear friend, unjustly and maliciously sentenced, and finally left to die high enough for everyone to see, naked on a cross – we would classify that as sexual abuse in today's culture. Even there, He was hated, ridiculed and misunderstood.

Why would the Father have chosen that kind of death?

A thought popped into my head as I was reflecting on this, again, while in Osaka, Japan, for a speaking engagement on reconciliation. Immediately, I knew the Source. "Derek, if it had been anything less, you'd be able to say, 'God, You don't understand what I'm going through.'"

The weight of the answer sunk into my heart. We can't say, "God, You don't know what it's like to be physically abused," or "God, You don't know what it's like to be lied about and betrayed," or "God, You don't know what it's like to experience the excruciating pain I've experienced," or "God, You don't know what it's like to be publically shamed, verbally abused and humiliated." The truth is this: He not only knows, but He has experienced it all Himself.

We have a Savior who is not distantly acquainted with our human condition, but who has experienced the worst of it. In experiencing such atrocities, He took the pains of our lives upon Himself. We no longer need to be victims; Jesus became the victim for us – and though we have been victimized, we are able to be completely restored.

Along those lines you may ask, "God, where were you when bad things were happening to me?" I remember asking Him that as I was walking through a restoration process in my own life. The answer came clearly. "Derek, I was in the same place for you as I was for my Son when He was hanging on the cross. I was present and I was grieving over the horrible decisions being made by people who were created in My own image."

God is present and God grieves.

"So?" I responded. "I was present and grieving, too." Actually, I think that many people in the world who do not know Him, see our Father in that light. They think He is a distant God who is present but distant … maybe grieving.

However, the Lord wasn't finished talking to me. He continued, "And, Derek, I was working – I was planning the resurrection. If you make the right decisions, you will discover resurrection instead of death!" Not only was God present and grieving, but He was actively working and planning my path to life again.

Jesus has experienced what we've been through – and much worse. He also showed us that *despite* what we have been through, when we make the right decisions under the cover of His grace and love, we will experience life. The greatest triumph is not in His death, but in His glorious resurrection! In this, we are shown that suffering is not the end. Instead, for all believers in Him, resurrection is possible. Jesus said in John 10:10, "I have come that they may have life, and have it to the full."

In all of our suffering, we can be assured about something we learn at the cross: God can bring to life treasures out from our sorrow. He can bring empowerment from our weaknesses, strategies from hopelessness, and resurgence from our confusion and loss.

## 5 | Discerning Truth

When mastering the art of question-asking, it's critical to understand that there are good questions and bad questions. Bad questions are typically rooted in false assumptions. If I were to go to someone and ask, "Are you still using illegal drugs?" that person is trapped in their answer. If they say "no" it implies they once used illegal drugs, but don't anymore. If they say "yes" they are admitting to being a user. The question makes an assumption ahead of time. A bad question often makes a false assumption. Truly devious and harmful questions are purposefully asked with malicious deceitful suppositions.

There is a question that has been asked by philosophers and intellectuals for generations – the fruit of which has been incessant, and often meaningless, dialogue. I think it is a bad question rooted in a false assumption. The question is, "What is truth?"

At first glance, the question seems to be a good one, invoking lots of spirited debate. But as the discussion rages on, people become confused and disillusioned as the logic of the question begins to break down. The key ingredient in making this question bad, is the false assumption that *truth* is a *what*.

When I was in college studying for one of my journalism classes, I remember learning the differences between *who, what, where, when, why,* and *how.* These are principle words for courses in journalism because any good news article must answer these basic questions in the minds of the reader. A news headline might read, "Five People Killed in Local Restaurant". The article will say, usually in the first few sentences, what happened, who was involved, where it happened, when it happened, and how it happened. It might read, "Yesterday evening, a purple SUV smashed through the walls of Sandy's Drive-In killing five people instantly and injuring twelve others." Then, as the article goes on, it will answer the *why* it happened. Maybe it was because the brakes had failed or the streets were icy. Maybe it was intentional and one of the people killed was an important political figure. But if they don't know the *why*, the journalist may write something like, "The SUV is still being investigated to determine the cause of the crash."

When learning about those different key words, we learn that the word *what* refers to an *idea* or a *thing.* So the question, "What is truth?" implies that truth is merely an *idea* or a *thing.* Current discussion of truth in the mainstream of unbelieving academia bears this out.

The famous Chinese philosopher, Confucius, believed truth was an idea – and not just an idea, but *his* set of ideas. He taught five basic tenets – common knowledge in most Asian cultures – and believed that should the community embrace these five truths, the society would be fine. Here is a list of them:

1.    Man is more valuable than woman.
2.    Older is more valuable than younger.
3.    The teacher is more valuable than the student.
       (Or educated people are more valuable than non-educated people.)
4.    The group is more valuable than the individual.
5.    Passivity is a virtue.

As nations in Asia embraced these ideas, the consequences have been catastrophic. Many women in those cultures grow up feeling horrible about themselves. They wish they were valuable men, instead of "worthless" females. Numerous younger people have been raised feeling oppressed, powerless, and looked down on by older generations. Uneducated people have felt inferior to educated people, though they may have far greater experience, knowledge or skills. These are individuals who feel repressed and rebuked by the group for daring to think outside the status quo. Regarding the fifth tenet, people can repress their emotions to unhealthy levels, yet feeling somehow virtuous that they do not display love, excitement, joy or anger. They remain entrenched in passivity.

Jesus actually acted oppositely to Confucius. He spent time with individuals, not just groups. He took the time to speak to women, affirming their intrinsic value. He championed children by telling His disciples that unless they become like a child, they would not inherit the Kingdom of God. We see Him display a wide range of emotions throughout the Bible and never being passive. Even when Adam and Eve had sinned, God took immediate action and came down to that Garden, calling out, "Adam, where are you?"

Finally, teachers are not more valuable in God's eyes than their students. They might be educated in a particular area or have more experiences in that area than most of their students. But suppose that a Cambridge University professor of Physics traveled to the North Shore of Oahu to try surfing for the first time. There is a good chance that professor would drown in fairly short order. Meanwhile, some local Hawaiians who may not have finished high school, could surf effortlessly through the largest and most dangerous of waves. Which one of those people is more valuable? Well, if I were surfing, my Hawaiian friends would be more valuable than the professor. If I had a question about quantum physics, a professor in that subject would be more valuable. Clearly, those basic beliefs of Confucius can be easily refuted.

If truth is not an *idea*, or a *set of ideas*, would it be a *thing*?

No, it would not.

There is a story of a lady in Hawaii who was convinced she could become one with nature and plug into the deeper consciousness of universal energy. She decided she would try to do this by meditating on a tree and repeating mantras to the tree. She was also an artist, so she would paint paintings of the tree, sculpt sculptures of the tree, make pretty *leis* from the blossoms and seeds of the tree, and drink soup made from boiling the bark of the tree. All day long she would hum quietly and try and be at one with the tree. One day, she heard a voice calling her by name, "Jackie." She turned around to see who had called her, but there was no one there. She heard the voice again a few minutes later, "Jackie!" Quickly she looked up, but there was nobody there. A third time she heard the voice, but this time it asked her a question. "Jackie, why are you studying the creation, when you can know the Creator?"

Something inside her jumped. She suddenly realized, "There is an *artist* behind the art!"

She got so excited, that she began asking everyone she met if they knew who made the trees. One evening, around sunset, she was on the beach and spotted a man with a beard and long hair. She approached him to ask her usual question, "Excuse me, do you know who made the trees?"

"Of course!"

"You do?" she began to get excited. "Does He speak? Can I hear Him?"

"Yes," he answered.

"Who is He?"

He looked straight at her and said, "God."

"How can I know God?"

Over the next few hours, he shared about how she needed to be forgiven from the sins in her life – the things that were holding her back from a healthy relationship with God and with people – and she needed to ask Jesus to come into her heart, cleanse her from her sins, and bring about a relationship with the Father Creator. So, this lady did all of that.

She did not find truth in an inanimate object. Truth is interactive, relevant and socially communicative. The tree had difficulty meeting that criteria.

Consider the enormity of the words of Jesus when He says, in John 14:6, "I am the way and the truth and the life. No one comes to the Father except through me." This changes everything!

Truth is not a what, but a Who. The person of Jesus is Truth! Truth is knowable, truth is interactive, truth is dynamic, and truth is applicable and pertinent, because truth is Jesus Himself. So our knowledge of truth is as profound, as intimate and as relevant as our relationship with Jesus. Truth is God's perspective on life. Truth is God's perspective on people and nations. Truth is God's perspective on family, government, education, economics and business, science and technology, counseling and healthcare, arts and sports, entertainment or communications, or religion. As we get to know the Truth, He fills us with the wisdom of our Creator for all areas of life.

# 6 | Restoring Our Identity

One of the beautiful discoveries we can make as human beings is to discover the Truth about *ourselves* – God's perspective on us. To do that, we turn to that great account of God and humanity revealed in the Bible. It begins with understanding how we were made. In Genesis, we read that God revealed Himself as light in the darkness, and then He created the expanse of water, the skies, the dry ground, the vegetation and plants, the stars and sun and moon, the living creatures flying through the sky, the animals on the land, and the life in the sea. He blessed it all and said, "Be fruitful and increase in number …" (Genesis 1:22). After that, He made humanity – both male and female – one not more valuable than the other, since both were made in His image (verse 27). It's encouraging to think that the first words ever spoken directly to humanity from God, the Creator, were words of blessing and provision:

God blessed them and said to them, 'Be fruitful and increase in number; fill the earth and subdue it. Rule over the fish of the sea and the birds of the air and over every living creature that moves on the ground.' Then God said, 'I give you every seed-bearing plant on the face of the whole earth and every tree that has fruit with seed in it. They will be yours for food. And to all the beasts of the earth and all the birds of the air and all the creatures that move on the ground—everything that has the breath of life in it—I give every green plant for food.' And it was so." (Genesis 1:28-30)

In the creation account we notice a difference between the "stuff" God had made (known as creation) and the human beings He made. Everything in creation was spoken into existence. God spoke and it came to be. But when He made humans, He did not speak them into existence. Instead, we read He formed man and woman with His hands. Genesis 2:7 reads, "The Lord God formed the man from the dust of the ground and breathed into his nostrils the breath of life, and the man became a living being." Adam was a highly designed machine of enormous potential, but lifeless, until God breathed His breath into him and he came to life.

Later, in Jeremiah 1:5, we read an interesting verse as God is speaking to the prophet. He tells Jeremiah, "I knew you before I formed you in your mother's womb." Again, we see God forming even the baby in the womb of the mother. But the exciting part here is about God knowing us before He formed us. It should not be surprising to us, and yet often it is.

When artists make their art, they don't just randomly construct it by throwing it up in the air and hoping it comes down as a masterpiece. It always begins with an idea. Artists, engineers, inventors, composers, writers, and architects, to name a few examples, are inspired by something they see, something they hear, or something they feel, and it *so* inspires them that they want to create. They think about it a lot. Then they to get to work. If they are sculptors, they begin to fashion the clay and mold it into a physical manifestation of the idea in their mind. If they are architects, they begin to sketch a drawing which, eventually, brings life to a building full of intrigue and expression. They might make some changes during the process, or add things after it has been tried out, but all of these artists have given physical expression to their original ideas.

It seems this is what God means when He says, "I knew you before I formed you." I think He was saying, "You were an idea in My mind before I began to put you together." He knew the personality He wanted to give us, the smile we would have, the sound of our voice, the music in our laugh, the color of our eyes, the size of our nose, the things we would be good at and the things we wouldn't be good at. All were part of a spectacular idea in His mind, conceived in a loving relationship between the Artist and His art, before He even formed us.

Like most artists, God loves His art. We are His prized composition – His favorite poem. In fact in Ephesians 2:10, we read "For we are God's workmanship, created in Christ Jesus to do good works, which God prepared in advance for us to do." The word *workmanship* in the Greek is the word *poemos*, from which we get the English word *poem*. We are God's living poetry.

A few years ago, while pondering these things, I was driving through the state of Virginia and had an opportunity to catch up with some friends I had not seen in a long time. I'd known them both when they were single and now they were married and had a four-year-old boy. We met at a restaurant and hugged each other before sitting down to look at the menu.

Suddenly, their little boy said, "Excuse me please."

We looked at him.

"Dad, I have a question. What does God look like? Because I used to know, before I was born, but now I forgot."

We were speechless. *What had this little boy said?*

I had just been thinking about Jeremiah 1:5 and how we were an idea lovingly conceived in the mind of God before He started forming us – and then this little boy pours these innocent words out of his mouth right into my heart. So I turned to his father and said, "Yeah, what does God look like?"

The father thought for a minute. Then he replied, "I'm not sure, son, but I bet you look a lot like He does."

He'd answered well, I thought. Yes, we are created in the image of God, our Father. We certainly must bear some resemblance to Him.

Through countless times of worship and prayer, King David understood this. He writes in Psalm 139:13, "For You created my inmost being; You knit me together in my mother's womb. I praise You because I am fearfully and wonderfully made; Your works are wonderful, I know that full well."

The idea King David conveys includes the intricacy with which we were designed. After all, knitting does not happen in a careless instant, but takes time, design and work. My friends, we were not a random act nor an accident. We were constructed after careful thought by our loving Creator God.

I was sharing this at a university on the West Coast of the United States that was known for its liberalism and atheism. As I spoke, a girl jumped up out of her seat to ask a question. "I'd like to believe all this – that I was an idea in the mind of God before He started to form me," she said with an edge of skepticism and hardness, "but I don't." She crossed her arms and glared at me.

Immediately, I could figure out some things about this young university student, although I'd never met her before. For example, I knew that she was not believing the truth. There are not many *truths* out there because there is only one Jesus Christ. Whether a person believes the truth or not, does not in any way change the truth. I could point to a car and say, "I believe this is an elephant." It doesn't change the fact that it is a car. Truth does not depend on its acceptance. Nor does truth vary from generation to generation to adjust to new trends or old cultures. Jesus is the same yesterday, today and forever (Hebrews 13:8). If this young student didn't believe the truth, then there was only one alternative. She believed a lie. And because she believed a lie, the other thing I knew about her, was that she was in darkness. John 8:12 reads, "When Jesus spoke again to the people, He said, 'I am the light of the world. Whoever follows me will never walk in darkness, but will have the light of life.'"

What I didn't know about her, was whether she loved the darkness or whether she just ended up there. One of the most famous verses in the Bible has to be John 3:16. "For God so loved the world that He gave His one and only Son, that whoever believes in Him shall not perish but have eternal life." There have been many sermons on this passage that focus on the word "loved". It comes from the Greek word *agape* and many pastors wax eloquently about it. They will say, "*Agape* is an unconditional love … a surrendered love … the deepest of loves … a sacrificial love …" And they are not wrong. That is what *agape* means and carefully used in this verse, we see it's the love God has for the world – for you and me.

However, in John 3:19, just three verses later, we come across the same Greek word for *love*. We read, "This is the verdict: Light has come into the world, but people loved darkness instead of light because their deeds were evil." Wow! Is it possible for people to have an unconditional, surrendered, deep, sacrificial *agape* love for darkness rather than light? Yes. This is why pacifism most likely will never work; there are people who love darkness rather than light.

I wondered, "Did this girl love darkness or was she just ignorant of the light?"

"It's okay if you don't believe this," I replied thoughtfully, "Can I ask you *why* you don't you believe it's the truth?"

She looked at me coldly. There was no doubt about her opposition to my message. "My mother was raped and I'm the product of that rape." She spat it out viciously. "Are you calling *that* God's loving plan and design? His great idea was for my mother to get raped?"

Suddenly, I understood her unbelief. I've discovered over the years that many people's skepticism is rooted in a deeply wounding experience. Maybe they were hurt by a pastor or church. Maybe specific Christians hurt them or their family. Maybe desperate prayers for healing or some other miracle had gone unanswered. Often these experiences lead people into a dark place, one of believing lies. She was asking a great question.

I looked at her for a few moments as she stood with her arms folded, her face darkened with anger, and her cynical eyes flashing.

"No," I responded gently. "God's plan was not for your mother to be raped. That is not at all like the character of God which we can read about in Exodus 34. However, your question tells me that you don't understand some important aspects about the cross."

"What do you mean?" she asked.

I shared with her the answer to the question, *Why did God choose for Jesus to die on a cross and not die from something easier?* And I explained about how the cross provided the answer to, *Where were you, God, when bad things were happening to me?* (We covered these answers in chapter four.) She flexed her jaw when I described how God was present, grieving and actively planning the resurrection, even in the midst of suffering and brutality. If the right decisions were made and the love of God was received, He could bring resurrection from what was meant for death.

She glowered at me in anger, but her voice betrayed desperation as she queried, "What was the life that came from my mom's rape!?"

I waited to respond, eagerly anticipating the work of the Holy Spirit, our Comforter and Counselor. The other students were waiting, too. *When we are in darkness, it's hard to see.* It was a simple thought, but profound enough to know it did not come from me. She actually couldn't see the light because she was in darkness. As Christians, we need to have lots of compassion for those who are in darkness; it is very hard for them to see.

Her question hung in the air.

"You."

I could visibly see the truth hitting her and spreading across her face. Tears, flowing down her cheeks, turned into sobs. All of her life she had believed she was the product of an appalling experience. The reality was God made a beautiful, intelligent, talented girl from that terrible rape. She was going to be the kind of woman who would be capable of loving and being loved, who would be a leader, regardless of the circumstances.

I continued to speak into the microphone the truth about her – God's perspective, taken from His Word. "You have been given life. You are His workmanship, formed by His hand. You are the resurrection from your mom's sadness."

After the meeting, she came up to tell me, "All my life I've been an atheist. I came to this school because I knew I would find allies. In this last half an hour, everything's changed! I don't know what to think anymore, but I know now … there is a God."

I nodded, "And He loves you very, very much."

The prophet Isaiah was right, "The people walking in darkness have seen a great light; on those living in the land of deep darkness a light has dawned." (Isaiah 9:2) When we have a paradigm shift like hers, it can be so unsettling. We realize that what we used to believe is not true at all. At that point, we are faced with hardening our hearts even more, or starting the rigorous humbling process of rebuilding our understanding of life from God's perspective.

A paradigm shift is a change in the way we see things. Often because of new information or something demanding a new perspective, our mind must adjust from how we used to think. It can be a very challenging process. On a smaller scale, think of a person you used to dislike, even though you'd never met them. Then, after you'd gotten to know them, you really liked them. This is a small paradigm shift – a change in your way of thinking about that person.

The disciples are good examples. They thought Jesus was going to overthrow the Romans and make Himself king. What a shift of thinking it took to realize the kingdom of Jesus was much greater and more encompassing than some variation of a worldly empire. We can look at Paul, formerly Saul, who was convinced he was doing the right thing by killing Christians. In one dramatic moment on the road to Damascus, in Syria, when he is asked by God, "Saul, Saul, why do you persecute Me?" (Acts 9:4) he discovered the very thing he thought was righteous and true was, in fact, a horrible mistake. God was saying, "When you persecute Christians, you are persecuting Me!" That is a terribly daunting thought, isn't it? Many Christians have even persecuted other Christians through the centuries simply because they baptize differently, structure their services differently, emphasize certain passages of Scripture over others, or celebrate communion differently.

Speaking of Saul on the road to Damascus, I need to interject something here. Some Christians get all amped up when they hear about "experiences" with God. They say, "You cannot base your theology on experience!" While I can understand their concern, I'd also warn them that Paul's entire theology *changed* after an "experience" with God. Isn't that something to ponder over? He certainly wasn't the only one in the Bible to whom we see that happening. I believe there are many Christians whose theology could use transformation even from one experience with the Almighty Creator God.

If we think about paradigm shifts on a broader scale, we might remember that some people were killed for insisting the earth was round. At that time, everyone "knew" the earth was flat. To say it was round was deemed to be heretical.

We can see that these kinds of shifts in our understanding are humbling. Often they are difficult to work through, sometimes painful or, in an extreme case, even deadly. But as we allow God's Spirit to guide us, we will discover such wonderful depth, precision and artistry to the designs and plans of God for each of us. When the intensity of the Holy Spirit hits us, we have a healthy, life-giving, enlightening paradigm shift. That university student in California was embarking on the greatest adventure of her life – the discovery of a loving God and His restoration plan for a fatherless daughter.

# 7 | Recognizing How God Speaks to Us

Our restoration comes because of one of the most amazing truths about God, the Creator of the universe: His desire is to communicate with people through the Holy Spirit, God's agent for communication. Paul writes in Romans 8:15-16, "For you did not receive a spirit that makes you a slave again to fear, but you received the Spirit of sonship. And by Him we cry, 'Abba, Father.' The Spirit Himself testifies with our spirit that we are God's children." Our spirit communicates with His Spirit and testifies to our relationship with the Father. We discover His inspiring love for us and our dynamic love for Him. The Holy Spirit can do this directly, by speaking to our minds or by interconnecting with us through insights or revelations from God's Word (the Bible).

Hearing the voice of God is not a difficult concept to grasp, although many people try to make it difficult. We don't see Ezekiel saying, "I think maybe God was speaking to me when He said to me ..." Instead we read Ezekiel writing, "He said to me, 'Son of man, stand up on your feet and I will speak to you.'" (Ezekiel 2:1) Noah wasn't confused about what God was telling him in the time before the flood. We read in Genesis 6:13, "So God said to Noah ..." and later we read in verse 22, "Noah did everything just as God commanded Him." Isaiah doesn't say, "I heard a voice and I couldn't tell whether it was God or my own thinking." Instead, in dozens of passages in this book, we read testimonies like Isaiah 5:9, "The LORD Almighty has declared in my hearing ..." After all, it would be a cruel cosmic joke if God created us for relationship, but never spoke to us. Isn't a key to a good relationship great communication?

Scripture actually doesn't record people struggling to discern God's voice; the struggle seems to be whether, or not, they should obey Him. In Exodus 15:26 we read, "If you listen carefully to the voice of the LORD your God and do what is right in His eyes, if you pay attention to His commands and keep all his decrees, I will not bring on you any of the diseases I brought on the Egyptians, for I am the LORD, who heals you."

Yes, it is possible to hear the voice of God and be obedient to His leading. We read that God spoke to Adam, He spoke to Noah, He spoke to Abraham, He spoke to Moses, He spoke to all of the prophets – even to the *child* Samuel and then He continued speaking to the *prophet* Samuel. He spoke to David and Solomon, He spoke to the disciples, He spoke to Paul, to Luke (neither one were part of 'The Twelve'). And He didn't speak to men only. God spoke to Hagar, He spoke to Sarai, He spoke to Miriam and Deborah

– just to name a few. Jesus talked with many women, including the distressed one from Samaria.

So, if God has spoken throughout all of history, to men and women, young people and older people, why would He stop speaking now? Why would God have suddenly changed?

A few years ago, I was in a large coastal city on the Eastern United States with some Christian friends and we were walking through a district of trendy bars. Suddenly, I had an urge to go sit at one with my friends. So I asked them to join me. While we were sitting there, a girl came and sat next to me. After some chit-chat, she said, "I've been speaking to God a lot recently." At this point I knew the urge I'd felt was from the Holy Spirit.

I turned to her and asked, "So what has He been saying to you?"

She looked slightly confused. "No, I've been speaking to Him."

I nodded, "So what has He been saying to you?"

"No – I've been the one talking to Him," she said with greater enunciation.

"I get it," I smiled, "But He talks back, you know?"

"He does?"

"Sure. That's kind of the point. You talk to Him and He talks back to you. It's a relationship, you know?"

She looked perplexed, took a sip from her drink and puffed on her cigarette. "Why haven't I ever heard Him?"

Now that's a great question. It is the question of a person who is keen to learn. It wasn't asked sarcastically – there was a genuine interest.

"Probably because you haven't recognized He was speaking to you," I answered.

Then a thought popped into my head.

"Close your eyes for a minute," I said.

She did.

"Now imagine that you are three years old." I paused, waiting for her to get the picture in her head. Then I said, "Imagine that you feel a tap on your shoulder and it's God."

Her face crinkled into a frown and I could tell she was rather nervous about an encounter with God.

I continued, "He says, 'Hey, I want to play a game with you. What game do you want to play?' Now just imagine playing that game with God."

After some time, her frown began to iron out and her face started to relax. With her eyes closed, she began to smile and smile. It seemed as if she was enjoying her time with God.

Finally, about five minutes later, I spoke quietly, "Okay, you can open your eyes."

They didn't open right away. Instead, tears began to form and trickle down her cheeks. She sighed and looked at me. "Wow."

I smiled, "How was it?"

"Amazing."

"What game were you playing?"

After a sip of her drink, she sat back. "I'm Japanese-Canadian," she began. "You probably wouldn't know the game – it is an ancient Japanese board game. What surprised me was how God and I were just sitting on the floor together. We were just sitting there, playing. I kept looking at Him, amazed that we were *sitting on the floor* together." In Japanese culture, the Emperor would never sit on the floor with common people, much less a child.

"As we sat there, we would move the pieces around on the board, each taking turns. I'd move my piece, look up at Him, and He would get this twinkle in His eyes, then move

His piece. I kept waiting for Him to get up and leave, but I had one hundred percent of His attention. I don't remember exactly what He looked like, but I do remember the feelings I got. He was very kind, full of love and peace. Sometimes God would look at me and smile. There was nobody else around, I have never felt so free of anxiety. It was the safest place I've ever been to."

"That's beautiful."

"I think it was the first time I've never been afraid."

I wasn't sure want to say, so I kept quiet.

"You have to understand," she continued. "My dad was never home. He was never there. He was always at work and I never saw him. Even on weekends. He was never by my door for me ... to protect my heart."

That was an interesting way to put it. Her dad was never by her door for her. He was never her heart's gatekeeper.

"As I got older, men would come in and out of my life, abuse me, and hurt me deeply – because I had no one by my door for me."

I was impressed with her lack of bitterness. She was just making a truthful statement.

"Why did you start to cry?"

"When you said, 'Okay, you can open your eyes.' I looked at Him and whispered, 'God, I have to go now.' And I'll never forget this as long as I live. God looked at me and said, 'Okay, Saki, but I want you to know something. I will always be by your door for you. I will never leave you.'"

Tears began to brim her eyes again as she looked at me excitedly, "I have a Daddy who is by my door for me!"

"Yes, Saki, you do," I replied.

"Can I do this again sometime?" she asked.

"Of course. He's by your door for you, remember?"

"Why haven't I heard Him like this before?"

How many people in this world are missing out on knowing God's love and faithfulness because they have never heard us tell them that God longs to communicate with His children?

I explained to her that people have hurt us, we have hurt others, and all of us have hurt God. This was how sin blocks our relationship with God. But when we ask Him for forgiveness and invite Jesus to come into our hearts, it opens our spirit-to-Spirit communication with God. It assures us of our relationship with Him.

"Can I do that right now?" She asked excitedly. "Can I forgive others and ask God for forgiveness?"

"Sure," I answered. And right there, she prayed a simple prayer of forgiveness, repentance and invitation. She is still talking and listening to God today.

As I've reflected on that night, I've wondered what would have happened, or not happened, had we ignored the thought of going into that bar with my friends. Many, who are stuck in legalism and fear, may have responded to that initial idea by countering it with, "I'm not going to go in there. What if someone recognizes me as a pastor? They might gossip about me or spread rumors about me." At some point, I think it's mature to live our lives in obedience to God with no fear of what gossipers might say. We want to honor God's desires and not our fears.

A few months after that experience, I was in my car, driving, and it suddenly dawned on me that I had never told her about heaven or hell. What a beautiful relational introduction to God she'd had.

As I thought more about it, I realized that often we can introduce God to people with a spirit of fear and say, "Give your life to God or you'll go to hell."

But is that how we introduce people to our friends? "Hi, this is my friend, John, and if you don't become friends with him, he'll blow you into oblivion with his arsenal of nuclear weapons. I hope you enjoy relating to him."

No, of course not!

Sometimes, it takes people a long time to overcome the fear of hell, instead of spending that time understanding the love of God.

That is not to say that there isn't a hell; I believe there is. And some people will go there, while others, who have accepted Christ's gift of grace, will not. After all, there were two men hanging on crosses next to Jesus and only one went with Him into Paradise (Luke 23:39-43). It's not to say that we shouldn't have a healthy comprehension of the greatness of God and our humble state before Him – certainly that is an important component of our perspicacity of God. But I think most of us would have loved to have met God through someone who just said, "Hi, this is God. He loves to play with you and has *so* desired to spend time with you – all your life actually. As you get to know each other, you are going to find out He loves you very, very much. There are lots of wonderful things God wants to share with you."

The Scriptures describes a number of different ways that God speaks to people. Sometimes He speaks through dreams, sometimes through angels, sometimes in an audible voice, sometimes through a vision, sometimes through other people, and sometimes through direct Spirit-to-spirit communication. His communication with people has never stopped.

My parents are godly people for whom I have tremendous love and respect. I remember, as a child, asking my mother, "How do I know I can hear God's voice?"

She smiled, "Because God's not a liar – and He says you can."

She was right.

We read it throughout Scripture. There are passages like Jeremiah 33:3, where God says, "Call to me and I will answer you." And there are scriptures like Hebrews 4:7, where it is recorded that King David said to the people, "Today, if you hear His voice, do not harden your hearts." And of course, she was right about God not being a liar. Numbers 23:19 reads, "God is not human, that He should lie, not a human being, that He should change His mind. Does He speak and then not act? Does He promise and not fulfill?"

There are so many real people in the Bible, many of whom we will meet in heaven, who've testified to hearing God's voice. King David, wrote in Psalm 86:7, "When I am in distress, I call to you, because you answer me," and the prophet Isaiah says in Isaiah 28:22, "Now stop your mocking, or your chains will become heavier; the Lord, the Lord Almighty has told me ..." Attend a church, go to a Christian bookstore, or even turn on a Christian television show and you will find many of God's children today describing similar experiences about hearing God.

Of course, when God speaks, He never contradicts Himself. What He says will always line up with His character and His ways, as we see outlined for us through the Word of God. If a man comes up to me and says, "God told me to leave my wife and live with a sixteen-year-old girl," I know that man has not heard from God. Our amazing Creator would not tell him to commit such a callous and selfish act of adultery. It would contradict what He specifically told us in His Word; it would devastate this man's life, the life of his wife, and the life of his family; it would cause almost irreparable pain in the life of the young girl; and it would cause confusion with non-Christians who aren't discerning enough to know what God would say to someone and what He would not say. God's voice will always line up with His character as it is clearly expressed to us in the Bible.

It's good to seek counsel, too, when hearing God. Proverbs 15:22 reads, "Plans fail for lack of counsel, but with many advisers they succeed." It's important to seek *godly*, wise counsel. Seeking feedback on important decisions from friends who have no fear of the Lord, nor a track record of making good decisions, is not a prudent idea. But asking friends who pray regularly, to pray with us as we are making important decisions *is* the kind of counsel we want in our lives.

When it comes to prayer and hearing the voice of God, I like the idea of *transfer*. God has an idea and then He *transfers* that idea to us during times of prayer, through the power of the Holy Spirit, so that we can think about it, strategize about it and act according to His will. One of my Australian friends described hearing God's voice as this: going into a meeting having an opinion about something, praying about that issue together, then, discovering that after the meeting his opinion had changed. Somewhere during that time of prayer, God had changed the thoughts of my friend to be aligned with His thoughts.

In 2003, I was part of planning an initiative we called the Wave USA. Frank Naea had just completed his term as the International President of Youth With A Mission, the world's largest interdenominational mission organization, and God was putting America on his heart. He'd invited me and a few others to get together and seek God about what we should do.

At first we thought we would just gather in Washington DC and pray for the United States. But gradually, as we continued to seek God, we began to understand that God's vision was much broader. So, then we thought we would intercede in Washington DC and also at the Cardinal Points of the nation. As we continued to pray, though, we realized it still wasn't enough. We needed to go to the whole of America. We came to realize that this journey was going include more than prayer. God wanted to show us things He was doing in the United States. He wanted to introduce us to ministries that nobody really had heard about, He wanted us to do evangelism, He wanted us to pray for people, and He wanted us to experience divinely set appointments if we would carefully listen to His voice and obey Him.

I still remember, as we were in an extended time of prayer as a group, Frank spoke out, "Fifty states in fifty weeks." Right away, it clicked with all of us. This was what God wanted us to do.

Two years later, we launched the initiative with people from many different nations. Sometimes we would know ahead of time what we'd be doing in the upcoming state ... and other times we had no idea. There were numerous times when we would drive across the border of a state, then we'd pull over and say, "God, here we are. What would You like us to do in this area?"

The whole time, God led us faithfully. At the end of the journey, we had hundreds of stories to tell about amazing people, wonderful things God was doing, how our faith and understanding of Him had been built-up, and how He was still working in the nation of America. We had been deeply encouraged and could testify of God's remarkable provision for all of our needs. By the time The Wave USA was finished, over sixty people had joined us on various parts of the journey for as long as they could and almost a third had gone to all fifty states. Most of the people were young and single, but we also had a lady who was in her seventies, a few married couples, and a family who had teenaged children.

When we were in Philadelphia, the team members of The Wave USA wanted to go look at the Liberty Bell. It is an iconic representation of freedom that gained tremendous importance when abolitionists adopted it as a symbol of their efforts to put an end to slavery in America. I had seen lots of pictures of the Liberty Bell and thought that was good enough for me, so I decided to find a parking spot for the shuttle I was driving and wait for them to come back.

After awhile, I decided I needed to go to Starbucks and get a vanilla latte with an extra shot of espresso. I locked up the shuttle, fed the parking meter and started walking. At that time, I didn't have a smart phone, so I asked God where a close Starbucks was. I have to admit that I didn't really know if He would speak to me. After all, does God really care whether or not I get my vanilla latte? As soon as I asked Him, a thought popped into my head, "Two blocks straight ahead and one block down on your left."

I remember a friend had once told me, "If you ask God to speak to you, be aware of the very next thing that pops into your head." So, I walked two blocks straight and then looked to my left. I could already see the Starbucks sign a block down the road. I made my way to it, opened the door and quickly noticed that there was only one comfortable chair that was unoccupied. I hurried over and put my bag on it, hopped in line, got my drink, and sat down.

Muttering to nobody in particular, I said, "Wow, it's cold outside!"

The man sitting in the comfortable chair next to me responded with a smile. "Where are you from?" he asked.

"Hawaii."

"Where in Hawaii?"

Now, I've learned that many people don't know enough about Hawaii. Most are surprised to discover there are multiple islands in our state. So I answered, "Kona. On the west coast of the Big Island."

He gave me a knowing smile, as if he knew exactly where I was talking about. "My wife and I have a condo in Kona. We go there every year for Christmas. What do you do there?"

That's an interesting question. I do lots of things. I'm a husband and father now – although during The Wave USA I was single. I pastored a church for ten years. I travel and speak when I get invited. I love to write. I compose worship songs and love leading people in worship. I have a passion for connecting people with God's nature and character. I love to travel and have a deep desire to see people from different nations and groups reconciled with each other. As I considered my answer, I decided to select the latter. "I work on international reconciliation initiatives in nations of conflict, specifically historical and generational conflict. What do you do here in Philadelphia?" I asked him.

"You are not going to believe this," he said with a grin. "But I am an attorney specializing in reconciliation among warring tribes in Namibia."

That began a friendship that has lasted for years. Sometimes, around Christmas, we would get together in Hawaii and talk about different aspects of reconciliation and how it impacts nations.

As I think about that day, I remember how hearing God's voice was as simple as thinking, "I want to go to Starbucks." Even the selfish idea of placing my bag on the one comfortable chair left in the café, seemed, in hindsight, to be the prompting of the Holy Spirit! I've often realized that hearing God's voice can be so uncomplicated that we often dismiss it.

We can see that kind of direct communication in Acts 9:10-12, right after Saul experienced his theologically transforming paradigm shift that we'd mentioned earlier. His eyes had been blinded, but God had wanted to restore his vision to him. He had decided to use a man named Ananias to accomplish that purpose. We read, "In Damascus there was a disciple named Ananias. The Lord called to him in a vision, 'Ananias!'

'Yes, Lord,' he answered.

The Lord told him, 'Go to the house of Judas on Straight Street and ask for a man from Tarsus named Saul, for he is praying. In a vision he has seen a man named Ananias come and place his hands on him to restore his sight.'"

As Ananias obeyed those specific instructions – albeit hesitantly, because of Saul's reputation for persecuting Christians – God used Ananias to restore Saul's sight. God spoke very specifically to both persons in this account. He didn't just tell Saul that someone was coming, but He had even told the apostle-to-be that the man's name was *Ananias*. This kind of communication with God happens best as we grow in our understanding and trust in the Lord.

## 8 | Relating to God from the Inside-Out

"How do we relate to God?"

I looked at the young man asking me the question during a train ride from Lausanne, Switzerland to Paris, France. I was on my way to speak at a convention and he was on his way back to university. We just happened to be in the same cabin and there were no other passengers with us. I had pulled out my Bible and was jotting down some things for my presentation the next day.

"Do you mean how do we start a relationship with Him?" I clarified.

"No. I'm a Christian, but I just feel like I have to work so hard at everything. Frankly, I'm burned out. There has to be an easier way."

I wondered where to go with this. "You're right. It can be exhausting. Particularly if we are caught up in the rules of the relationship more than enjoying the Person in the relationship."

"What do you mean?"

I put away my Bible, notebook, pen, and computer, and got a cup of coffee from the passing snack cart.

His question was a good one. And this would take time.

It's interesting that the first miracle of Jesus was to turn water into wine. I would have thought an interesting foreshadowing would have been to raise a person from the dead or heal a group of lepers. But turning water into wine? What's even more puzzling are some of the components of the event itself.

The details are chronicled in John 2. Jesus, His mother and His disciples had all been invited. A crisis came up – as they often do during weddings – and this one was that they had run out of wine. This was a problem. People usually gave their gifts and money to the bridal couple on the last day of the wedding. If the wine ran out, many would probably leave early and the couple wouldn't get much money on the last day. I imagine there may have been the usual complainers who would have caused a scene had they known there was no more wine left. Now, apparently in the Hebrew culture of the time, if a single guy brought wine to a wedding, he was announcing that he was ready to find a bride. So, being a good Jewish mother, Jesus' mom told him, "They have no more wine." Not ready for a bride, because the bride was not ready for Him (that would be *us* by the way, *the church*), Jesus told His mother that His time had not yet come.

Were I to lead a Bible Study on this passage and then ask people to find the key verse, many would point to the very next verse – where the mother of Jesus says to the servants, "Do whatever he tells you." That is a good idea for us, as servants of God, to do whatever He tells us. It's definitely a good statement to reflect on. Another key verse they might find would be where the master told the bridegroom, "You have saved the best until the last." (2:10) Maybe it would encourage us to know that the best is yet to come. We could get hope from that. Some people might say verse eleven. "What Jesus did here in Cana of Galilee was the first of the signs through which He revealed His glory; and His disciples believed in Him." Honestly, that verse used to puzzle me a bit. How did making lots of wine reveal the glory of Jesus?

To me, the key verse is one not usually picked. Verse six reads, "Nearby stood six stone water jars, the kind used by the Jews for ceremonial washing, each holding from twenty to thirty gallons." Now why would this be a key verse? Is it because of the amount of wine? One hundred and eighty gallons would certainly be an impressive amount of wine. But I think the key is in the *kind* of water Jesus used. He did not turn ordinary drinking water into wine, although that would have been the logical choice. Instead, he turned the water that the Jews normally used for ceremonial washing. It was the nasty water they would stand in front of and dip their dirty hands and arms into – all the way up to their smelly armpits. Then, they would shake it off as a sign that they were ceremonial cleansed. It meant they had no communicable sicknesses that could affect others since they had been ritually cleansed. We read that the master of the banquet "did not realize where it had come from, though the servants who had drawn the water, knew." The poor guy might have had a coronary, knowing that his guests were sipping filthy water now called wine.

Why would Jesus have chosen that particular water? I think it revealed the entire ministry of Jesus. He was making a foundational statement. John specifically tells us that this was the first of the signs "through which He revealed His glory."

He was saying, "No longer are you going to be cleansed ceremonially on the outside by unclean water, but you will be cleansed by My pure blood – from the inside out!"

The Gospels of Mark 14:24, Matthew 26:28, and Luke 22:10 all record that Jesus said, after what we call the *Last Supper*, "This cup is the new covenant in my blood, which is poured out for you." So we see the connection: wine representing the sacrificial blood of Jesus.

This new relationship with God begins from the inside – in our thinking and emotions – and not from outside ceremony. Some people get so caught up in religious activity (the outward show) that they are emotionally and physically exhausted while their hearts are shallow and their minds are spiritually immature. Then there are some, who might show virtually little outward religious activity, and yet have an amazing depth of spiritual character emanating from the inside – where the Holy Spirit is truly at work.

While being a part of a team that was leading worship in New Zealand several years ago, wonderful things happened. After seeking God about the upcoming time of worship, we decided to use all of the arts. So, we had paint and easels in the back, clay and a potter's wheel, a dance floor, spots for people to preach or teach – even if it was just to an empty wall. We encouraged everyone to worship God with all their heart and giftings, in any way that suited them. Of course, music was a big part of it and I was playing the keyboards as others played different instruments. Truly, it was an incredible time. One lady testified later that, as she had had her hands in clay, for the first time in her life, God spoke to her and said, "This is the feeling I had in my hands when I was forming you!" She just wept as she realized that she had not been quickly formed in a whim, but that there had been a lot of planning put into her design.

One person stood at the back just watching everything. He had dark sunglasses on and folded arms across his chest.

"What a sad thing." I thought. "He's missing out on all the fun."

During a musician's break, I decided to talk to him, "So. How was the worship time for you?"

"It was great!" he said to me, not noticing my *exhorting* attitude. "I walked into the room and God just spoke to me — really clearly, you know?"

I raised my eyebrows.

"He said, 'Brace yourself like a man; I'm going to speak to you.' It's kind of like what He said to Job, right."

I nodded.

"So … I've just been standing here and He's been speaking to me. It's been awesome. I've been thinking about the greatness of God. It's amazing how He can be worshipped in so many different ways. Why don't we do this more often? It's so cool to apply all of the arts in worship, so dynamic. It's just multiplied so many ways to connect with God!"

I was more than embarrassed. I had judged his outward activity instead of trusting that God was working on his inside.

He wasn't finished. "There is such a strong presence of God here, don't you think?"

"Yes".

"I've never seen anything like it. Have you done this before?"

"No," I mumbled. "We had been praying about this worship time the other day and one of the ladies on the worship team felt like God wanted to do something new."

He smiled, "Well, it definitively triggered something new in *my* heart! Thanks so much."

I went back to the keyboard, repenting to God for the attitude of my heart and determining in my mind to think differently next time.

On another occasion, I was speaking on Biblical Principles for Business to a group of entrepreneurs in Singapore. I had arrived a day early to adjust to jetlag and decided to stroll down by the beautiful river-walk area. I found a place along the water to eat, and as I started into my chicken and rice, I noticed another single man across from me. After he had finished his meal and paid his bill, he stopped by my table.

"I don't think you know me," he said. "Most people around here do."

"I don't."

"I own a large Karaoke bar just down the street. Come by if you'd like – it's lots of fun."

"Thank you," I said politely, thinking there were many things I'd rather do, but already knowing I should go there to understand why God would bring this man across my path.

When I walked in, someone was singing on stage. I was amazed at how large the bar was and at how packed the place was. I'd only been there a few minutes when the owner I'd met walked over, shook my hand and stuck a microphone in it. "Welcome! It's great to see you. You'll sing next." He flashed a big smile.

I grew up singing, so I wasn't too intimidated by the thought, and browsed through the song book. There was nothing in it I cared to sing.

And that's when a still, small, recognizable, voice inside me said, "Derek, I want you to sing something *a capella*. I want you to sing *Pour Out My Heart*." I pondered the thought. I knew Craig Musseau's song well enough, but singing with no back-up instrumentation to a very crowded bar would most certainly make me stick out rather than blend in.

The owner returned with another smile. "So, what song are you going to sing?"

"Um. I think I'll sing something without the background music – just *a capella*."

He looked at me, flabbergasted. "We don't usually do that."

I wasn't surprised.

After a brief moment, he'd made a decision, snagged the microphone, held it up to his mouth and with his free hand motioned to everyone in the bar. "Ladies and gentlemen! Please! Quiet down! We have a very special moment today. A remarkable singer has stopped by tonight and would like to perform a song – without the background music. He has come all the way from Hawaii and I would like for you to put your hands together for Derek!"

Good grief.

I managed a smile as he handed the microphone and winked. "Good luck."

The lyrics are simple, but poignant:

*Here I am – once again*
*I pour out my heart*
*For I know that You hear every cry*

*You are listening*
*No matter what state my heart is in*
*You are faithful to answer*
*With words that are true*
*And a hope that is real*
*As I feel Your touch*
*You bring a freedom*
*To all that's within*
*In the safety of this place*
*I'm longing to*
*Pour out my heart*
*To say that I love You*
*Pour out my heart*
*To say that I need You*
*Pour out my heart*
*To say that I'm thankful*
*Pour out my heart*
*To say that You're wonderful!*

A hush came into the bar as the presence of God began to settle in that place. I sang it through one more time, smiled, and gave an awkward bow.

For a few seconds the room stayed quiet and then suddenly it erupted into applause. People said things like, "That was powerful," or "Your voice is amazing!"

I had to grin. My voice is average. But the voice of the Holy Spirit can be like a rushing wind! We're powerless in and of ourselves, but greater is He that is in us than he that is in the world (John 4:4).

One man pulled me aside later, and enquired. "Can I speak with you?"

"Of course."

"I know that song."

I wondered where this was going.

"I used to go to church," he said, almost wistfully, "they used to sing that song there."

Immediately, I knew he had been hurt. This was not a thought from me, but from our loving, heavenly Father. "You've been deeply hurt by that church, haven't you?"

He nodded.

"I even think it was a pastor who hurt you. I am so sorry." I continued, "Listen, the whole reason God brought me to this place was to let you know – He is less interested in your going to church, than He is in a real, honest relationship with you. When you go home, why don't you try to rediscover the love of God? Just start a conversation with Him."

He thanked me and gave me a big hug as I left.

Should he go to church? Maybe – when he's ready. More importantly, shouldn't he go back to our loving Father who has been waiting for His child to come back home? God is mostly concerned about the work going on *inside* our temple for the Holy Spirit. (I Corinthians 6:19)

There is a wonderful lady in one of the world's most difficult red light districts. She had decided that since the prostitutes there all want to get their hair, nails and make-up done, she could start a salon in the middle of the area to reach them with the love of Jesus. So she did. She has been working diligently in that ministry for forty years and loves to share about the days when she first started.

"I wanted all of them to get to know Jesus as soon as possible," she recounted to a group of us. "So, I'd tell them about Jesus and talk them into leaving their life of prostitution. Many of them did ... but all of them were back on the streets several months later. It was very depressing."

She went on to tell us how one night, she had a dream in which she heard the voice of God call her by name, "Why are you so impatient with these girls? Why don't you have the same patience with them that I have with you?" Immediately, she was convicted, realizing that God had always been very patient with her. Not being able to fall back asleep, she opened her Bible to 1 Timothy 1:16, "But for that very reason I was shown mercy so that in me, the worst of sinners, Christ Jesus might display his immense patience as an example for those who would believe in him and receive eternal life." She knew she needed to change her approach.

Over the next few years, she patiently loved the girls, building a relationship with them, and helping them out of difficult situations whenever she could. "Now, it takes a girl about three years, from the time she first enters the salon, to give her life to Jesus," she told us. "It takes another two or three years for her to leave prostitution. Over the last thirty years, we have had a one hundred percent success rate. Now, when they leave that life, they never go back."

It takes these women time to learn about God as their Father. Often their own fathers were the ones who sold them into prostitution. How would God protect them, when no one had? Would God provide for them, as well as their families? God – our Healer and Restorer – was patient with them, gently revealing Himself to them one step at a time. After a period of time, confident in their relationship with God, the Holy Spirit would nudge them to leave their life of sin (John 8:11). And they did.

It seems that though Jesus introduced the new covenant relationship with God, many people are still living off the old covenant. Covenant speaks specifically to how we relate to

God and how He relates to us. It speaks of a system for relationship.

Under the Old Covenant, only the priest could represent the people before God. Only the high priest could repent before God on behalf of the nation. Hebrews 5:1 tells us, "Every high priest is selected from among the people and is appointed to represent the people in matters related to God, to offer gifts and sacrifices for sins."

However, when Jesus was hanging on the cross, the curtain in the temple was miraculously torn into two parts. This was not just an ordinary veil. We read about it in Matthew 27:51 and Mark 15:38. It was a thick curtain that separated the Holy of Holies from the rest of the temple. The Holy of Holies was the place where the high priest could meet with God. No one else was ever permitted entrance. Once a year, on the Day of Atonement, he was allowed to enter to ask God for forgiveness on behalf of the nation. He would offer incense at the entrance and the blood of the sacrifice before the mercy seat, which was part of the ark of the testimony (Exodus 26:33-35 and Hebrews 9:3,4).

When the large dividing curtain was ripped from top to bottom, as Jesus expired on the cross, a violent earthquake rattled the land because God was making a dramatic change. At that moment the entire earth became the Holy of Holies! No longer was it relegated to a little space where only the priest and God could meet, but now the whole earth was a place where people themselves could meet with God and dialogue with Him. This fulfilled a prophecy in Habakkuk. The prophet wrote "For the earth will be filled with the knowledge of the glory of the Lord as the waters cover the sea." (Habakkuk 2:14)

Under the New Covenant in Christ, we read in Hebrews 4:14-16 and in Hebrews 8:11, that all of us can now know God and interact with Him because Jesus became our high priest and mediates on our behalf. There are a lot of people who look to their pastor as a type of high priest. They depend on their pastor for spiritual nourishment and wait for the pastor's interpretation of Bible passages to decide what to believe. They look to their pastor for help in times of crisis and financial disasters, and they often lean on their pastor when they are going through times of sickness. They forget that neither a pastor nor a priest is our intermediary.

Sacrifices, in obedience with the Old Covenant commandments, served a purpose. There was the shedding of blood, but in that process there was a deeper significance. Hebrews 10:3 tells us that the sacrifices were set up as a continual reminder of their sins. Every time they saw a sacrifice it was like seeing a crucifix – they were faced with their sinful state and their need for God's forgiveness. Under the New Covenant, we read in Hebrews 8:12, the grace of God says, "I will remember their sins no more." What an amazing thought! The Almighty God, who could keep a very specific record of wrongs for each one of us, has decided that if we apply the blood of Jesus to our lives and repent of our sin, we will not only be forgiven, but God, our Father, will remember our sins no more.

One final aspect of the difference between the two covenants is that the Old Covenant was written on tablets of stone (Exodus 31:18) whereas the New Covenant is written on our hearts and minds (Hebrews 10:16). This difference is very important. It helped me form an answer for the young man on the train who had asked me about how we could relate to God.

"It's true even in our own lives," I told him. "Sometimes our focus needs to be less on the outward action and more on the condition of our hearts. This is the place where God is wanting to bring peace, healing and restoration. Eventually, over time, we will see the fruit of the ministry of the Holy Spirit in our lives, as well as in the lives of those around us."

## 9 | Worshipping Our King and Dad

It's quite astonishing that as individuals, we can interact intimately with God. Very few of us have ever met a real king or queen on this earth. Yet, each one of us is able to have personal conversations with the Creator of the heavens and the earth! He is greater than any king, of course! He is the King of kings and Lord of lords; He is the great Almighty God; He is the Beginning and the End – the Alpha and the Omega. There is no one like our God. So, how is a personal interaction made possible with this God?

I've been privileged to visit a lot of nations and wherever I go, I see differences. These are not bad things. North Americans might say that the British drive on the "wrong side of the road." Yet, in Britain, it is the correct side of the road, so perhaps it would be better to say that the British drive on the "opposite side of the road." When traveling, it's good to keep in mind *different* is not necessarily *wrong*.

We see some stark differences in how people relate to God, too. Some people think our relationship with God should be formal because He is the Almighty One. I had a biology professor like that in college. When he spoke to students, he used current, informal English, but when he was praying, he would communicate in the English of Sir William Shakespeare. It used to bother me until I decided to enjoy the difference. Certainly God could understand both Old English *and* street English.

Many of my Asian friends get confused by our Western informality in communication with God. To them, "Hey, God! What's up?" seems like an unfitting way to start a conversation with the Almighty. They may be right.

Sometimes, it would be good for many of us to slow down and picture ourselves entering into the throne room of God. It would be the most exhilarating place we had ever seen or imagined. There would be millions of people from hundreds of nations, some of whom we never knew existed, standing before the throne worshipping God in their own language. Instruments we'd never seen before would be playing. People would be dressed in bright, national regalia. Angels would be circling everywhere crying out, "Holy, holy, holy is the Lord God Almighty, Who was, and is, and is to come!" Jesus Himself would be sitting at the right side of the Father's throne and near Him you might hear the songs of "Worthy is the Lamb who was slain – to receive glory and honor and praise!" Your eyes might be drawn to certain individuals and suddenly you might see your great-grandfather. Next to him might be one of your best friends from high school. Suddenly, the music stops. The chanting fades. The light from the throne becomes a spotlight on you. Every person, every creature, Jesus and the Father are listening to the next words that come out of your mouth. What would your opening words be, in the presence of billions of witnesses and the Most High?

There is protocol to meeting with the King of kings and the Lord of lords – the God above all gods and Maker of all. Thankfully, the Bible is full of verses instructing us in that protocol. Protocol is a system of formalities and etiquette that creates welcome, provides structure, and opens doors into the heart of a person or nations. If we were to have dinner with the Queen of England, we'd have to get trained in how to eat correctly, how to sit, how to address her when we'd like to speak and how to present our gifts. The same thing is true if we were to meet with other leaders of nations. Protocol shows respect for the other person's culture, which includes greeting, giving, and receiving. In Hawaii, if you greet a lady, you kiss her once on the check – usually the left side to the left side. In Japan, this would be highly offensive, but you would bow. In Asia, bowing is the appropriate greeting, but the bow is a slightly different from nation to nation. In France, you'd kiss a friend on both cheeks. In other European nations, you would use hearty handshakes.

There is protocol, as well, for presenting our requests before God. In Philippians 4:6, we read, "Do not be anxious about anything, but in every situation, by prayer and petition, with thanksgiving, present your requests to God." So we should not just barge into the presence of God with whatever we think is so important. Instead, we need to take the time to come with *thanksgiving* – having a grateful heart! This is like Psalm 100:4,5, which instructs us to, "Enter His gates with thanksgiving and His courts with praise; give thanks to Him and praise His name." Why? The Psalmist tells us, "For the

Lord is good and His love endures forever; His faithfulness continues through all generations."

Another protocol verse is from Psalm 24:4, where we are told to come before God with "clean hands and a pure heart." That's a good idea! The writer here is referring to the works of our hands – our deeds – and our heart, or our motivations. What is our true motivation for coming before God? Are we coming with a pure heart?

Psalm 95:6 reminds us to "bow down in worship" and "kneel before the Lord our Maker." Many times in my own life, things suddenly lost their urgency after I bowed before God and worshipped Him. Paul writes in Romans 14:11, "It is written: 'As surely as I live,' says the Lord, 'every knee will bow before me; every tongue will acknowledge God.'" When King David instructed his people to praise God, we read, "So they all praised the Lord, the God of their fathers; they bowed down, prostrating themselves before the Lord and the King." (I Chronicles 29:20)

People have told me, "But I have the freedom to worship God however I want!" That statement is true – surely. But what is freedom? Is it the "right" to do whatever we want?

No, freedom does not mean we can do whatever we want.

Let's say, for example, that I were to walk up to a guy, hold a knife to his throat and say, "I want to kill you."

Most likely he would object. He might say something like, "No! Please don't kill me; I don't want to die."

I could argue with him and say, "But I'm free – I can do whatever I want – and right now, I want to kill you!"

Now we have a problem. Hypothetically, of course, I want to kill him, but he doesn't want to die. We need a law!

What law could possibly help us? What about a law that says something like, "You shall not murder?" That's a great idea. That way, the person I'd been threatening is free to live and I'd be free to work on my issues.

Of course, that's a ridiculously extreme analogy, but it speaks to how freedom is not a green light for lawlessness. It is not a "get out of jail free card" for doing whatever we want to do, or saying whatever we'd like to say.

As a matter of fact, freedom requires law. I like to say that freedom is our ability to live in healthy restraint. There are restraints that are not healthy – from unjust laws, to prejudicial treatment of people groups, to the oppression of women or the abuse of children. Those restraints are warped and flawed. They should not be a part of a free society. But healthy restraints give *life* to a community. They allow people the liberty to plan, work and live in the safety and protection of just laws.

Did you know that every just law in society can be traced back to the character of God? We certainly have the freedom to make our own choices. Hopefully, we also have the wisdom to make the right ones. Theologians call this freewill. It's something God created in us because we are created in the image of God – and He has freewill.

When I work with worship leaders, I usually say something like this, "You have the freedom to lead worship with whatever song, whatever style, and whatever instruments you'd like to use. However, remember, you are not building a worship service for yourself or even for people like you. You are leading a diverse, multi-cultural, multi-generational group of Christians and even non-Christians. Your mandate is to lead all of them into worshipping a holy God. You will need to figure out how to include everyone and how to move them forward in worship."

Think of the account in Luke 15:11-32 which we have called the story of the Prodigal Son. The younger son demands his inheritance and tears out of his father's house on a reckless and wild rampage, blowing his entire fortune. If we were to interview him prior to his leaving home and ask him to define freedom, he would say, "Freedom means I can do whatever I want. I'm finally out from the rule of my parents. I can finally spend *my money* the way I want. I'm ready to live *my life* the way *I feel* like living it!" How many college students do we know with that same perspective? How many teenage runaways have those same devastating ideas?

In Jesus' narration, the young man finally has nothing left and accepts a job to feed some pigs – a despised animal in Jewish culture. We read that he "longed to fill his stomach with the pods that the pigs were eating, but no one gave him anything." He had spent all of his inheritance and had not one single friend left.

If we were to ask him to define freedom at this point, it would no doubt be a very sobering answer. He would probably think about it carefully and say, "Living at my father's house in the provision of his love. That was freedom." Some people live in abusive homes and leaving them is truly a step toward their freedom and wholeness. But Jesus gives this illustration as an insight into how much God loves us. He tells us that even when we stray and make a myriad of stupid choices, God passionately yearns for us to return home. As a matter of fact, the young man finally makes a good decision and chooses to return to his father's house – even if it means living there as a servant. The father, however, sees him from a distance, runs to embrace him, and welcomes him as his long lost son.

We can't stop God from loving us, but we can cut ourselves off from receiving His love by our own stupid decisions. A helpful analogy might be to imagine a miserably cloudy, rainy day. It's cold outside, wet and generally depressing. If this weather were to continue for weeks, we'd get to the point where we'd wonder whether or not the sun was even shining – we'd longingly recall the days of the sun on our faces and the warmth in the air. The clouds are like sin and unbelief in our lives whereas the sun is like the love of God. When we align ourselves with who God is, through the power of the Holy Spirit and the Word of God, the rain stops, the clouds part, and we realize the sun has always been there for us. His love has always been radiating from Him and we are able to receive His deep affection into our hearts in a life-changing way.

Protocol helps us remember that God is God and we are not. We bow before Him, we sacrifice and give to Him, we pledge obedience to Him, we offer our lives to Him, we do His will and we are on His side. In Joshua 5:13-15, just before the Israelites attacked Jericho, Joshua encountered a man standing in front of him with a drawn sword in his hand. This would be the equivalent of walking around the corner and seeing a man with a pointed gun. Joshua asks him, "Are you for us or for our enemies?"

Now, if ever God was for the Israelites, it would have been at this point, wouldn't you think? They were getting ready to step into fulfilling the covenant of God to Abraham. They were preparing to cross the Jordan River and take the land God had promised to Moses. They were determined to move from being wandering slaves to becoming a nation of landowners. Of course, God must be for them!

The man looks at Joshua and answers, "Neither."

Neither? Joshua learns an important lesson here. God is not on *our* team, we are on *His*. God is not necessarily for *my* project, *my* career, or *my* ministry. I am here for *His* work – His projects. My friend, Jeff, pointed out to me one time, "A servant doesn't set the agenda for the master – the master sets the agenda for the servant."

The man continues, "As commander of the Lord's army, I have now come."

In other words, "I'm here because I'm the commander of the Lord's army and He has assigned me to come – not due to your *own* good plans, Joshua."

Joshua falls facedown to the ground. He understands the situation and asks, "What message does my Lord have for his servant?"

The message from the commander was a simple one. "Take off your sandals, for the place where you are standing is holy."

Isn't that odd? Not really. Joshua is reminded of the time God was calling Moses. At this point, in this generation, Joshua was just another leader in the continuum of God's plan. He was encouraging Joshua to remember that the land was not his, but our Creator's. David writes in Psalm 24:1, "The earth is the Lord's, and everything in it, the world, and all who live in it ..." What a great reminder to Joshua as he embarks on moving forward with the plan of God!

Here is what we learn from all of this. After our protocol, God responds. He runs to us and speaks into our ears, whispering, "You can just call me *Dad!*" Is that not an amazing answer to our etiquette? We know this is true because Jesus instructs His disciples to pray, "Our Father in heaven ..." He doesn't tell them to say, "All Powerful Being – Father of Jesus." Instead, we can say, "Our Father." What a privilege. In Mark 14:36, Romans 8:15 and Galatians 4:6, we read that we can just excitedly call out, "Daddy!" or if we speak Hebrew, "Abba!" or if we speak Korean, "Appa!" There is no other god like our God. He is perfect in all of His ways.

As I have reflected on this over the years, I realize that for most of us, in our devotional times, our worship times, our prayer life, we often choose to remain in the place of protocol – a place of respectful distance from the King of Kings and Lord of Lords. On one hand, our worship needs to include the protocol aspects of relationship to God. But on the other hand, it should also include our childlike excitement and delight in calling our majestic Creator, "Daddy!" This is why Jesus allowed the children to come to Him. He doesn't favor children over adults, but He was modeling the Father's response to us – His children! Jesus says in John 14:9, "Anyone who has seen me has seen the Father." As the children were welcomed around Jesus, so we are welcome before our loving and faithful Father.

# 10 | Identifying the Work of Jesus

Being before God as children and expressing childlike love for Him is only possible because of the *work of Christ*. Without His work, we would be standing before God, in the area of protocol, with fear and trembling.

Ephesians 2:11-22, tells us that Jesus is the one who made peace between us and God. He "destroyed the barrier – the dividing wall of hostility – by setting aside in His flesh the law with its commands and regulations." The apostle Paul goes on to write that, "You who once were far away have been brought near, by the blood of Christ," and later adds, "Through Him we both have access to the Father by one Spirit. Consequently, you are no longer foreigners and strangers, but fellow citizens with God's people and also members of His household."

Jesus came down to earth and lived a remarkable life. He fought through the temptations presented to Him by our enemy and was sinless – meaning He was without sin – up until the moment He was on the cross. Even then, He did not sin, but exercised His freewill and chose, out of obedience to the Father, to take *our* sin upon Himself. We read "God made him who had no sin to be sin for us, so that in him we might become the righteousness of God." (2 Corinthians 5:21). As we mentioned before, at that moment, as Jesus experienced the separation that sin causes between us and God, the Father. He cried out, "My God, my God, why have you forsaken me?" Jesus experienced our problem, first hand. He experienced what eternal rejection from Father God – the penalty of our sin – would be like for us.

His life was powerful. In Luke 3, Jesus was baptized in water and we see the Holy Spirit descend on Him in the form of a dove (in Luke 3:22). He leaves the place of baptism full of the Holy Spirit. Luke continues (chapter 4) that Jesus was "led by the Spirit" into the wilderness to be tempted by the devil. Imagine that? Often, after an experience with God, we think that our career is going to shift into high gear, where we see God doing amazing things through us, but instead we find ourselves in the wilderness. In that scorching desert, we can get hungry, become thirsty, find ourselves susceptible to confusion, and be brutally assaulted with temptation from our enemy. It can leave us reeling from the situation and wondering what happened.

Luke narrates how the devil spoke out his temptations three times and how Jesus responded to each occasion. Then, we read that the, "devil had finished all this tempting" and left him until "an opportune time." Note verse fourteen, "Jesus returned to Galilee in the power of the Spirit ..." So we can see that the progression is from being *full of the Holy Spirit* after baptism, to being *led by the Spirit into the wilderness*. And only after victoriously and tenaciously continuing, Jesus emerged *in the power of the Holy Spirit.* His model of obedience to the Father demonstrates that when we successfully endure the wilderness, full of the Holy Spirit and led by the Spirit, we can emerge in the power of the Holy Spirit!

Not only was the life of Jesus powerful, but it was also identificational. He "shared in our humanity," as we read in Hebrews 2:14, and His life is an example to us. Who better to model being human than Jesus? Want to know how to handle criticism? Study Jesus. Want to become a better question asker? Study Jesus. Want to know how to handle those who knowingly cling to sin? Study Jesus. Want to know how to better relate to the Father? Study Jesus. How to relate to each other? Study Jesus. We could go on and on, but suffice it to say, that the life of Jesus is our best example of how to live as a human being. Want to know how to suffer? Study Jesus. Because the work of Christ also includes His death – a brutal, humiliating, abusive death – the kind happening in many parts of the world today and one that could easily happen to us as the times get darker.

I was in Jerusalem by the Wailing Wall – the last remaining wall of the ancient temple – standing next to a young Orthodox Jewish couple from New York. We chatted a little bit and talked about different things relating to Jewish custom and the nation of Israel. All of sudden a question popped into my head.

"Whatever happened to the sacrificial system?"

The young man nodded and said, "Well, we believe the sacrifices need to be made in the temple – but since we have no temple, we can't offer sacrifices."

Another question came to mind, "So how do you know whether or not you have been forgiven of sin? Wasn't the forgiveness of sin always accompanied with sacrifice?"

He nodded, sadly. "That is the true theological dilemma of the Jewish person. We really don't know whether or not God forgives us. There is a prayer we pray in the Talmud that says, 'Forgive us of our sins,' but we know forgiveness is always accompanied with sacrifice."

What a precarious position for this young Jewish couple.

Isn't it wonderful to know that Jesus became the sacrifice of all sacrifices? That with His death, the sacrificial system ended? Jesus, the Lamb of God, offered Himself as a sacrifice for us all.

Yet as significant and identificational as His suffering and death were, they would have been for nothing had it not been for the astonishing resurrection of Jesus. He rose from the dead and conquered it all – letting us know that when we suffer and when we go through pain, there can still be victory at the end. When we make the right decisions, to obey God and walk in the power of His resurrection, He can turn our mourning into gladness and give us comfort and joy instead of sorrow (Jeremiah 31:13).

The final part of the work of Christ is still ongoing. People may think that Jesus' life, death and resurrection sum up His work, but there is still an important role being taken up by Jesus. I love what Job writes. We can hear the cry of his heart as he considers the condition of humanity:

"God is not a mere mortal like me that I might answer him, that we might confront each other in court. If only there were someone to mediate between us, someone to bring us together, someone to remove God's rod from me, so that His terror would frighten me no more." (Job 9:32-34)

Job is crying out for a mediator! Little did he know that thousands of years later, Jesus would come to earth, experience our condition, die on the cross, and rise triumphantly to become exactly what Job is envisioning – our Mediator. 1 Timothy 2:5 reads, "For there is one God and one mediator between God and mankind, the man Christ Jesus who gave Himself as a ransom for all people." It is significant that Paul writes, the *man* Christ Jesus. It is precisely because He came as a *man*, and identified with our *humanity*, and shared in *our* suffering, that He understands His mediating work on our behalf. And because of Jesus, Paul is able to write in Ephesians 3:12, "In Him, and through faith in Him, we may approach God with freedom and confidence."

What does all of this mean? As followers of Christ's example, we too should live a life worthy of our calling. In the might of the Holy Spirit, we can emerge from our wilderness experiences with power. We need to carry our cross and surrender in obedience to God, the Father. Remember, it was Jesus who said, "Whoever wants to be my disciple must deny himself and take up his cross daily and follow me." (Luke 9:23) Then, there is resurrection life available for us. Romans 8:11 reminds us, "And if the Spirit of him who raised Jesus from the dead is living in you, he who raised Christ from the dead will also give life to your mortal bodies because of his Spirit who lives in you."

Emulating the life of Christ seems easy, in theory, but isn't it much more challenging in practice? After all, the same enemy that opposed Jesus also opposes us – the people created in the image of God. In his passion to destroy the work of God, he relentlessly attacks us and we battle against him daily.

## 11 | Detecting the Enemy

In our uber politically correct society, it almost seems inappropriate to think any harsh warlike thoughts about a being. But truthfully, we can never think harshly enough about our enemy. 1 Peter 5:8 reads, "Be self-controlled and alert. Your enemy, the devil, prowls around like a roaring lion looking for someone to devour." And in John 17:15, when Jesus prays to the Father before going to the cross, He says, "My prayer is not that You take them out of the world, but that You protect them from the evil one."

One thing about our enemy is that he doesn't just want to tempt us. We can have a tendency to fixate on how he tempts us and how we try to overcome temptation. Certainly there is no problem with that – he does tempt us and we need to fight against it. However, our enemy is interested not merely in tempting us, but he wants to *destroy* us. Temptation is never his end game – only a means to the end. His goal is our total destruction. Our enemy wants to destroy our marriages, our families, our friendships, our relationships at work, our involvement in the community, interactions between roommates, our churches, our nations, our system of relating to other nations and even our lives. He will do whatever it takes to wreak havoc in our lives. In our fight against our enemy, it's good to think beyond specific temptations and dwell more thoughtfully on how succumbing to temptation would lead to our destruction. Peter writes that our enemy is looking to devour us – not just to lure us into a snare – but literally, shred us to the point where there is nothing left.

Jesus says of our enemy, in John 8, that he is the *father of lies*, a *murderer from the beginning* and a *robber who comes to steal from us*. He also says that there is *no truth* in our enemy. Jesus, being the Truth, can easily recognize there is no truth in the enemy – not even a little bit of truth.

That statement by Jesus bothered me for many years – not because there was anything wrong with it, but because I struggled to grasp the full idea. Wasn't there a *little* bit of truth in our enemy? After all, in my own life, when the enemy would tempt me, often he would tell the truth about some sin in my past or something that I should feel ashamed about, and then he would try to beat me up with it. He doesn't just make up stories or accuse me of things I haven't done. Instead, he uses things from my past that are factually correct and then drives the condemnation deep into my heart. I'm sure his strategy is the same for you. He always brings up something we *really did do*, something we *really did think*, or something we *really did say* that was hurtful. The sins he reminds us of, in the theater of our mind, are things of which we really are guilty. Even though we have asked God for forgiveness, the enemy still tries to use our past words and actions against us.

What about when Satan was tempting Jesus in the wilderness? We can read about it in Matthew 4 as well as in Luke 4. Was the devil not quoting Scripture? Isn't Scripture truth? He wasn't twisting the Scriptures or misquoting the Scriptures, nor was he manipulating them. He was quoting them verbatim. So, is it that there's just a *little* bit of truth in the enemy?

No. Not according to Jesus. He said there is *no truth* in our enemy. None. He said in John 8:44, "He was a murderer from the beginning; not holding to the truth, for there is no truth in him. When he lies, he speaks his native language, for he is a liar and the father of lies."

To better understand this, we must pursue the Word of God deeper. When we do, we find there are passages like 1 Corinthians 4:5, saying that God "will bring to light what is hidden in darkness and will expose the motives of men's hearts." Proverbs 16:2 says, "All a man's ways seem innocent to him, but motives are weighed by the LORD." Wow! So, God not only judges our actions and words, but even our motivation.

For further clarity, we can look at the sin of gossip. Gossipers think their gossip is justified because the juicy tidbits of information they are passing along are true. They might gossip about someone, and then if caught and confronted, respond by saying, "Well, what I said was *true!*" Before God however, they will be judged not just by whether they were lying or not lying, slandering or not slandering, but instead by the *motivations of their hearts.* Proverbs 11:13 says gossip is linked to "betrayal" and Proverbs 16:28 says it "stirs up conflict and separates close friends." Paul includes people who gossip with people who are filled with "every kind of wickedness, evil, greed and depravity," in Romans 1:29-31. He writes that these people are, "… full of envy, murder, strife, deceit and malice. They are gossips, slanderers, God-haters, insolent, arrogant and boastful; they invent ways of doing evil; they disobey their parents; they have no understanding, no fidelity, no love, no mercy." Yikes! Gossip is a serious matter because it has to do with the motivation of our hearts and not just the veracity of our claims.

Most gossipers operate out of deep feelings of inferiority, unforgiveness, or a strategic desire to "take someone down." Those motivations are rooted in fear, leading to control.

Some time ago, I was flying from a country in the Middle East to a nation in Europe. As people were boarding the plane, a lady took the empty seat next to me, wearing a black burka that covered her from the top of her head to her toes. I was intrigued and really wanted to ask her some questions about her Islamic faith. I love asking questions and learning. But, I also knew it might be inappropriate or even dangerous to talk to a Muslim lady as a white non-Muslim man. I didn't want to offend her or get her in trouble.

As I was deciding not to talk to her, she suddenly turned to me and asked, in perfect Queen's English, "Excuse me, are you a Christian?"

I tried to mask my surprise at her accent and her question. "Um, yes, I'm a Christian," I stammered, "Are you, uh, Muslim?"

She laughed, "Obviously!"

"Your English is very good."

"Thank you," she said. "I actually live in London where my father is a doctor and where I grew up. I was just visiting family and now I'm flying back to London."

"Oh, that makes sense."

"So … you *are* a Christian?"

"Yes," I said.

"I have a question for you."

I had to chuckle inside. I'd been thinking about asking her questions, but she had a question for *me*.

"What does the Bible have to say about love?" she asked earnestly.

What an amazing question! I could hardly wait to answer it. But before I did, I quickly asked God for His wisdom to answer her with His thoughts.

"That's a great question. The Bible really has two things to say about love," I started. "The first thing, is that God is love. 1 John 4 actually mentions it two times. Love is the fabric of God's character and the foundation of all He does and says. It doesn't say that God is *like* love or that God merely feels love; it says He, in fact, *is* love."

She nodded, attentively.

"Secondly," I continued, "The opposite of love is not hate. As a matter of fact, hate seems to be an important part of love."

She tilted her head, wondering how hate could be a part of love.

"The apostle Paul wrote a letter to the young church in Rome. In the Bible it's called the book of Romans. We read in Romans 12:9, 'Love must be sincere. Hate what is evil; cling to what is good.' So in order for our love for God to be sincere, we must hate what is evil. This doesn't mean we hate people or people groups, but we should hate evil. And then we should cling to, or grab without letting go, that which is good."

"What is the opposite of love, then?" she asked.

"The opposite of love is fear. In the same chapter where we read that God is love, we also read in verse eighteen that, 'There is no fear in love. But perfect love drives out all fear.'"

She exclaimed excitedly, "That makes perfect sense! Perfect sense."

"It does?" I said, a little surprised – although I don't know why I should have been. There is power in the Word of God – it is a light to our path (Psalm 119:105).

"Yes, it does." She sat back and shifted her body to look at me, her dark eyes flashing with excitement. "You see, I have always wondered why I have such a hard time giving and receiving love from people. In the past few months, it has bothered me more than ever. I'm not just talking about boy/girl relationships. I mean with all of my friends. I have a hard time receiving their love or generosity, and often I feel like I'm very guarded in expressing my love or appreciation to them. But now it makes *total* sense."

She paused for a moment and I waited for her to finish, not wanting to interrupt this moment of truth-filled revelation for her.

"I grew up in a typically Islamic family. My father is a really good man. He has been a steady provider, but he was also very, very controlling. So in my family, where I should have been learning all about love and having loving relationship in a *safe* environment, I was actually learning fear. Fear ruled our home. We all tread on eggshells around my father – so afraid to set him off. So now, whenever I try to give or receive love – even in the smallest of ways – there is actually fear in my foundation. I think fear must be the root in every one of my relationships."

I looked at her, my eyebrows raised, "Most people I know wouldn't connect the dots in their lives so quickly."

"I graduated from Oxford University when I was sixteen and completed medical school by the age of twenty-one."

She sighed happily and I had to smile. She was a smart lady who just had a Holy Spirit-inspired paradigm shift.

Going back to our enemy, the devil, what is his motivation? What is the motivation that would cause Jesus to say he had *no truth* in him, even when he was quoting scripture?

Satan's motivation is the opposite of the motivation of God: God is motivated by love and freedom, while Satan is motivated by fear and control. Whenever Satan is attempting to bring us down, discourage us, or ultimately destroy us, he's bringing up things in our past that are factually correct, but because his motivation is evil, Jesus could confidently declare that our enemy is the "father of lies" and that there is "no truth in him." When Satan was tempting Jesus, he was trying to cause a fear-of-Satan, rather than a love for God. He was attempting to control the Son of God. But Jesus was unfazed, knowing his motivation.

You might be thinking of your life at this point, or even about the general body of Christ. By and large, do we operate from a foundation of love and freedom or do we operate from a place of fear and control? It's certainly something to think about.

## 12 | Overcoming Fear

Since that conversation on the plane, I've thought a lot about fear versus love. Fear is first mentioned in the Bible at the very beginning, as we read about the story of Adam and Eve. After Adam had sinned, God came down to the garden. In Genesis 3, He called out to Adam and said, "Where are you?" Adam's response was typical of many who enter God's presence. He replied, "I heard you in the garden, and I was afraid because I was naked, so I hid."

God calls out, but Adam says that he heard Him, was afraid and so he hid. For the first time in the human relationship with God, we see fear. I don't think we were ever designed to be afraid of God. We don't see fear before the Fall. Fear is a characteristic in our own personality that we cannot find in God.

Now, someone might ask, "What about the fear of the Lord?" Certainly the fear of the Lord is real. We see Isaiah deeply worried in the presence of God because he came from a people of unclean lips and was guilty himself (Isaiah 6). But God extended forgiveness to him and his guilt was wiped away – his sin was atoned for. As a matter of fact, many come into the presence of God with fear, but He always encourages them to not be afraid. It's my opinion that the fear of the Lord is the consequence of sin. Had Adam not sinned, we would not be afraid of God.

What was Adam afraid of? I believe it was a manifestation of our deepest fear. He was afraid of being rejected by God. Many researchers tell us that the greatest fear in people is the fear of death. But why are they afraid to die? Could it be that many are really afraid of standing before God when their lives will be bare before Him? Or, have they chosen to ignore what He has revealed about Himself and are now afraid of the consequences of that decision?

Not only did fear enter the relationship between God and humanity, but fear entered all inter-human relationships at that time. Fear causes many kinds of pain through the way people relate to each other. Whether it be a fear of judgment by others, fear of failure, fear of rejection, fear of completing things, fear of trying something new, fear of letting go, fear of being misunderstood, fear of authority, fear of making the wrong decisions, or any other kind of fear, we can literally be paralyzed by it.

There are great examples of people in the Bible who reveal this to us. Peter, for example, was out in the water all night and not catching any fish. We read in Luke 5, that Jesus told Peter (at that time we know him as *Simon*) to let down the nets for a catch. Of course, the fisherman, exhausted from a night of fruitless work, objected at first, but conceded, "… because you say so, I will let down the nets." They caught such a large number of fish that their nets began to break!

Now wouldn't you think, after such a marvelous encounter with Jesus, that Peter would be super excited? Instead he reacted like Adam. He fell down before Jesus and said, "Go away from me, Lord; I am a sinful man." I'm sure we've all felt that way at some point in our relationship with God. We can relate to being so full of condemnation and shame that we want to push God away, and not stand in His glorious presence. How do we conclude that Peter was expressing the same fear that Adam expressed when he was "afraid" and "hid"? From the very next sentence! Jesus responds to Peter and says, "Do not be *afraid*."

There are many Christians who depict Peter to be some kind of foot-in-the-mouth, bumbling clown. But nothing could be further from the truth. Peter was a hard-working, small business owner in a very competitive line of work. As a matter of fact, he even tells Jesus, "We've worked hard all night and haven't caught anything." Anyone who knows commercial fishermen knows they often fish for long periods, sort their catch, transport them on ice (back in those days, probably cold water), and then sell as many fish as they can, early in the day. On top of that, they are always fixing their boats, mending their nets, trying to out-pace their competition and are very dependent on the weather. It's hard work and never stops because people are always hungry.

Maybe Jesus chose Peter because he was a strong leader who was not afraid to speak his mind. For certain, Jesus wanted to use Peter's giftings. "Fishermen understand how to fish," my brother (who loves fly-fishing) pointed out to me one day. "They understand timing; they understand baiting; they understand preparation and planning; they understand lakes, rivers and oceans; they know currents and weather patterns; and they recognize seasons and how to read the signs of nature." It was precisely those giftings that Jesus wanted on his team. After Jesus encouraged Peter not to be afraid, He told him, "From now on, you will catch men." (Luke 5:10)

Much later, we read about Peter's painful betrayal of His Master. It certainly is a dark moment in the life of this bold disciple. Afterwards, he was out there weeping *bitterly* (Matthew 26:75 and Luke 22:62). I wonder what was running through his mind. Perhaps he was remembering when he first met Jesus. He may have been sitting there thinking, "I knew it. I knew You should have never called me to follow You. I knew I'd mess up. I knew I was a sinful person ... I knew I'd fail." Before you think I'm reading too much into this, remember that Peter was a young man very much like us. The enemy used the same tactics back then that he uses today. He would have dragged out all of the same condemnations, "You're no good, Peter. You're a failure. You let Jesus down."

Peter leaves the place where he was weeping to return to what he knew: fishing. At this point in the story, you're wondering what on earth is going on. Peter had just spent a few amazing years with Jesus Himself! He'd seen Him heal the sick, give sight to the blind, feed thousands with a few loaves of bread and two fish, raise people from the dead, forgive people, and he spent countless hours absorbing the wisdom of God and putting it to use. Yet, here he is on the lake, fishing, as if nothing had happened. We read at the beginning of John 21 that Peter had told Thomas, Nathanael, the sons of Zebedee and two other disciples, "I'm going out to fish." Next thing you know, they all decide to go back to fishing, "We'll go with you."

You know something? I want to march right up to Peter and ask him, "Do you think that Jesus picked you, walked with you, talked with you, and showed you astounding miracles just so you can go back to doing the same old thing you were doing before?"

Again, we can most likely see ourselves here. Maybe there were times when God moved in our lives, and instead of pressing into what He had for us or risk obeying Him further, we just returned to what we knew: the same old routine as before. I see it at youth camps and church retreats. People have a "moment" with God where they are completely humbled and moved by His Spirit. They make promises and commitments to God which they fully intend to keep. However, later, under some kind of pressure or misguidance, they go back to doing the same things they were doing before – as if nothing had happened – and often with the same group of people in their lives. It must break the Lord's heart.

In an amazing passage recorded for us in John 21, Jesus uses the moment in a beautiful way. It seems the whole chapter is about Peter and his restoration. Remember, we had learned earlier that God has unlimited power to create and to restore. And as it unfolds, the story seems like a déjà-vu. We read it and think, "Haven't we already read this?" Peter and the disciples are out on the lake fishing and they aren't catching anything. So Jesus urges them to cast their nets on the other side of the boat – it's a very similar story to the one in Luke 5. Is this a mistake in our Bibles? Did John get his facts mixed up and insert the story in the wrong chronology? Of course not. There is something much more precious and wonderful going on here. Out of His love for Peter, Jesus is recreating the whole story of when they first met. It seems He is setting a stage that Peter recognizes. And so, as the disciples obey Jesus, they end up catching 153 large fish. They are so excited; they even count every fish!

After they come to the breakfast Jesus had cooked for them, Jesus turns to Peter. In verse fifteen, Jesus asks him, "Simon, son of John, do you love me more than *these*?" Unfortunately, our English versions miss something here that is better understood in the precise Greek language. The word "these" does not agree in gender, number and case with the disciples. The only possible thing it could agree with is the fish Jesus was grilling on the fire.

Jesus was asking Peter, "Do you love me more than these *fish*?"

What a game changer! Fishing was the safe and predictable lifestyle Peter had returned to and also a passion of his. It was how he provided for his family and the community – it was his livelihood. People knew Simon as *the fisherman* – it was even his identity. Now Jesus was asking him whether or not he loved Him more than his fishing career?

What a great question! What about us? Does Jesus ask us whether we love Him more than *the fish* in our life? What would the *fish* be for you?

Jesus was not against fishing or He wouldn't have helped them get some big catches. What He was gently asking Peter had to do with Peter's priorities. Jesus died for people. He came from heaven for people. He came to save and redeem people – not jobs, nor passions.

Several weeks later, note the exciting moment for Peter, recorded in Acts 2. Empowered, equipped and emboldened by the baptism of the Holy Spirit at Pentecost, Peter gets up in front of the crowd. We can see his leadership and his giftings as a fisherman in full display. He delivers a speech by setting the stage, baiting the people, and casting the net. The tension builds up as he declares, "Therefore, let all Israel be assured of this: God has made this Jesus, whom you crucified, both Lord and Messiah!"

The people hear this and are "cut to the heart". They desperately ask, "Brothers, what shall we do?"

Peter pulls in the net, saying, "Repent and be baptized, every one of you, in the name of Jesus Christ for the forgiveness of your sins. And you will receive the gift of the Holy Spirit." The net swells and bulges ... and about three thousand people respond. It's the greatest catch of his life! The loving prophetic words of Jesus must have been ringing in his ears, "Do not be afraid. From now on you will catch men."

Yes, perfect love drives out all fear. The love of Jesus dispelled the fear in Peter. It freed him to fulfill his destiny in Christ.

Another example, in this context, is Moses.

If you read your Bible, you know his story from the first part of the book of Exodus. He was born into a tumultuous time in history. The Israelites had been in backbreaking, cruel slavery to the Egyptians for over 400 years. They had been crying out to God for freedom – not unlike the trafficked slaves of today, I'm sure. In spite of the heavy persecution, their families stayed intact and their population kept growing. The Egyptian Pharaoh worried that the slaves were becoming too numerous, so he instructed the midwives to wait until the child was born, adding that, "Every boy that is born you must throw into the Nile, but let every girl live." In Exodus 1:15, we read, "The midwives feared God and did not do what the king of Egypt had told them to do; they let the boys live." What courage these women displayed!

When Moses was three months old, his mother put him in a tar-coated basket made from reeds and sent him down the Nile in a last-ditch effort to save his life. The little baby boy floated right to the place where Pharaoh's daughter was bathing. She opened the basket, saw the baby, and decided to raise him as her own son.

As an adult prince in the castle, while he was out and about one day, Moses noticed an Egyptian beating up a Hebrew. He looked to the left and to the right, and seeing no one, he killed the Egyptian and hid him in the sand. Of course, the news of what he had done had traveled to Pharaoh, so the king of Egypt tried to kill Moses. At that point, even though he had been raised in the king's palace, we read that Moses was *afraid*. He ran far away from Pharaoh to live in Midian, where he ended up tending sheep for forty years.

In Acts 7:25, we read, "Moses thought his own people would realize that God was using him to rescue them, but they did not." This is thought-provoking because it tells us that even *before* God called Moses to lead his people, he had a pretty good clue that his destiny was to be involved in freeing the Israelites from slavery. Otherwise, why would he have killed the person who was wronging a Hebrew? However, despite knowing his calling, Moses fled from Egypt to Midian. This is the same spirit of fear we saw in Adam; the same fear that haunted Jonah, the prophet; and the same fearful response we see many centuries later in Peter. It may even be the same fear we recognize in ourselves.

While Moses was sitting there with the sheep, he might have been doing what a lot of us do. He might have been rehearsing all his failures on the grand stage of the theater in his mind. He might have been looking a sheep in the eye and telling it, "I used to be a pretty big deal. I even grew up in the courts of the greatest king on earth. Did you know I'm an Egyptian history scholar? I can speak several languages. I used to be really good at what I did. Everybody looked up to me. But boy, did I screw *everything* up!" His mind would have gone back to those few minutes of idiocy when he killed the man, hid him in the sand, and ran away, scared.

Forty years is a long, long time. Then, one day, Moses was out walking around his sheep when he spotted a fire in the hills. Knowing a fire could rip through the whole area and cause all kinds of damage, he climbed up there to investigate. Oddly, the fire was not consuming the bush. And at that lonely mountain spot, God meets Moses and speaks to him personally and very clearly, calling him to lead the people of Israel out of slavery.

In the Bible, we find lots of good examples of how to respond to God. Isaiah hears the voice of God in Isaiah 6 and responds by saying, "Here am I, Lord, send me!" That is a good response. In chapter three of 1 Samuel, we read of a little boy who hears the voice of God, audibly, calling his name. He responds with, "Speak, Lord, for your servant is listening." That too, is a good response. When Ananias, in Acts 9:10, hears God calling him by name in a vision, he responds by saying, "Yes, Lord." A great response.

Moses did not have a very good response. He begins shoveling the objections at God, even claiming that he was, "slow of speech and tongue." We even see Moses shifting from hesitancy, to attacking the character of God. He is actually indicating, "Creator God, you made a mistake when you thought I should be the one to lead these people out of Israel – I'm not even a good communicator."

Here, the Lord gets a little perturbed. He responds by saying, "Who gave human beings their mouths? Is it not I, the Lord?"

But Moses was a very stubborn individual, even among the sheep. In that sense, wouldn't he be the perfect person to lead this huge group of people? In his desperation, he dug in and we read in verse thirteen that he finally said, "Please send someone else." What a miserable response to the call of God.

This story of Moses is brought up again in Acts 7:20-22, where we read about the stoning of Stephen, but with a very interesting twist. Just before they throw the rocks at him, Stephen takes a moment to retrace the history of Israel in order to testify of Jesus. When he gets to the part about Moses, he reveals, "At that time Moses was born, and he was no ordinary child. For three months he was cared for by his family. When he was placed outside, Pharaoh's daughter took him and brought him up as her own son. Moses was educated in all the wisdom of the Egyptians and was powerful in speech and action."

What? Stephen declares that Moses was *powerful in speech and action.* But Moses claimed he was *slow of speech and tongue.* Those are polar opposites! Which one was he? Was he powerful in speech and action or slow of speech and tongue? Either this is an example of an inconsistency in Scripture, as some people like to label it and are ready to toss the whole book out, or there is something else happening. I believe it's the latter. My conclusion is that Moses, having spent forty years tending sheep as a foreigner and having rehearsed his failures over and over, had long ago given in to a spirit of fear. The shepherd Moses lived with a perspective of himself that was *not* the perspective God had of him. He truly believed he was slow in speech in tongue and not the right candidate to lead the Israelites out from Egypt. But God was seeing the man He had created him to be – the one who was powerful in speech and action. And we know, from following the life story of Moses, that he was indeed powerful in both speech and action. Never once do we see him slow of speech and tongue. Whether he was speaking in front of the great Pharaoh, speaking in front of the Almighty God, or addressing the people of Israel, he always knew what to say and how to say it.

Fear can cause us to actually have the wrong viewpoint of our lives, our talents and our future. When we look back to the moment when Moses told God to go and pick someone else, it is absolutely staggering to think of what he was unknowingly ready to give up. He was willing to give up his calling, his inheritance, the freedom of his people, and his own family's destiny in God. All this, because he was afraid.

Fear can paralyze us. It can keep us from our destinies. It can steer us away from the new things God would have us embark on. It can keep us trapped in a stifling routine that can lead to our death – whether physical death, like a suicide, or the death of dreams that God placed on our heart. Fear can control us, consciously and sub-consciously. We end up carrying that fear into our families, and extending it into friendships and people with whom we interact. As a result, some people continue to sit on the hillside with the sheep, rehearsing their past, rather than obeying God and taking radical steps forward.

Paul writes, in 2 Timothy 1:7, "For God has not given us the spirit of fear, but of power, and of love and of a sound mind." (NKJV) Different versions of the Bible have different expressions of the words in this verse. The New Revised Standard Version, for instance, uses the word *cowardice*, in the place of *fear* and some versions say *timidity*. So the spirit of *fear* is not from God – it is not something He equipped us with.

The *power* that enables us to overcome fear does not come from ourselves, but from God. We read about it in Romans 8:11, where we are reminded that the Spirit of God lives in us. The same Spirit that raised Christ from the dead, in fact, "gives life to our mortal bodies through His Spirit." The only question is this: do we submit ourselves to His power and guidance in our lives, or do we let the spirit of fear continue to control us? I think that when we read "God has not given us a spirit of fear," He means it. If we are enslaved to fear, then we really don't know the *power* and *love* of God.

The other component mentioned in fighting against fear is a *sound mind*. It is amazing how illogical fear can be. I remember when a friend of mine almost drowned. The person who jumped into the pool and saved his life, grabbed him and just stood up! As it turned out, all he had to do was stand up because he was already in the shallower end of the pool. God actually gives us a sound mind when we learn His thoughts and are able to adopt the mind of Christ (1 Corinthians 2:16). Some of us might think we are drowning because of the attacks of our enemy, when we only need to stand up and seek the face of our Savior.

Remember how we mentioned 1 John 4:18? How perfect love casts out, not just *some*, or a *few of*, but *all* fear? Our complete security is in His love for us – it overcomes all fear. Our complete wholeness is in the fact that He promises He will never leave us or forsake us. Some of us are convinced that we cannot fulfill the commands of Jesus, the calling of God in our lives, or the plans He has for us. But, as we discover the security of His love, the wholeness of His faithful companionship, and the deliverance that comes from trusting Jesus, we can walk away from fear.

Fear leads to control, which eventually leads to legalism and religion. But the love and freedom that flows from God, can lead us into intimate, wholesome, fruitful relationships – with Him and one another.

## 13 | Thieving and the Power of Words

We've just learned that the intent of our enemy is to destroy us and that his motivation is one of fear and control, but Jesus also called him a *robber* who wants to steal from us. Fear can actually open the door to thievery. This is an interesting matter. A retired police chief explained to me that there are three categories to consider when things have been unlawfully taken from you. There is burglary, which involves breaking into a building without consent from the owner and with the intention of committing a crime inside. There is theft, which is taking something from someone else with the intention of permanently depriving them of it. And finally, there is robbery, which requires both theft and a form of violence, or a threat of violence, to deprive someone of their property. Jesus says in John 10:10 that the *robber* comes to "steal, kill and destroy." Our enemy does not only steal from us, but he has the violent intent of destruction.

In the midst of all this, we realize our life is not a battle as much as the battle is for our life. There is always an attempt by our enemy to steal the good seed that is being planted in us and it is being done violently, without any regard for our wellbeing. He attempts to rob us of our intimate relationship with God and he attempts to keep us from understanding the love of the Father. When that happens, we become hardened to the grace offered to us in Jesus and we can systematically destroy our relationships with people. This is not a battle about our salvation; we may have already given our life to the Lord. But how we live out our salvation in our daily lives, and whether or not we will fulfill God's designs for us, is in a constant battle. Our enemy knows that if he can steal our intimate relationship with Jesus, he is making giant strides towards derailing the fulfillment of our destiny according to God's plans.

Besides our intimate relationship with God and people, what other things does our enemy, Satan, steal from us?

He tries to steal our perspective on truth. We have already talked about how truth is not a *what*, but a *Who* – the *person of Jesus Christ*. So truth is Jesus' perspective on all of life. Nowadays, the lies thrown at us from all angles come in the form of opinions. It's important for us to recognize that everyone has a right to an opinion, but not every opinion is right. In many nations, everyone not only has a right to an opinion, but they can blog about it, post it on social media, put it into newspapers, journals, books, movies – the list goes on and on. Everyone can do that – they are free to do that in most of our nations and have the right to do that. But that freedom doesn't mean that their viewpoint is necessarily correct or true. In today's tsunami of social media opportunities, we are being absolutely inundated with people's opinions. And most of these views seem to be held next to the Word of God, not under it.

Suppose someone came out with a breakthrough story in the *New York Times* about an amazing discovery. It went on to tell how Nobel-winning scientists had just discovered a purple Siamese ant from which all of life began. Wouldn't there be lot of Christians who would say, "How wonderful! We finally know where life began!" You see, many would rather give credence to some kind of opinion in the New York Times, or whatever other source, than to trust the account given to us by our Creator God. Think about the result of the enemy's thievery at work to color our perspective on Truth. We will end up actually believing deceptions. With our poisoned minds, we easily compromise what we read in the Word of God and gradually, we even doubt the veracity of the character of God.

At that point we have doubted His Word, we have doubted His character, and so we doubt Him with our decision-making. This is the strategy employed in Genesis 3, when the serpent came to Eve and told her, "Did God *really* say ..." He wanted to create a seed of doubt in her mind on whether or not God really spoke the truth. Was that what God had *really* said to Adam? Had He *really* heard God clearly? Lack of this trust makes us become suspicious, fearful, and isolated people. Our communication with God becomes superficial and powerless. Jesus pointed this out in Matthew 22:29 when He told the compromising Sadducees, "You are wrong, because you know neither the Scriptures nor the power of God."

Another piece the enemy likes to steal is our love for God and our passion for His personality. We can easily become more absorbed by our own interests instead of God's interest and we can stop caring for the needs of others. Today, when we read, "Love your neighbor as yourself," we just read it as saying, "Be sure to love yourself before you try anything helpful." I don't know how many books I've read where the writers say that we should focus on ourselves, loving ourselves, and taking care of ourselves. Is that the impression we get from Jesus? I've actually found that when I focus on helping others and giving to others, I get healed.

Sometimes the enemy likes to attack our security and peace. He creates an anxiousness in us. We conclude that prayer doesn't really work. God would surely not be interested in listening to us with all the major crises in the world. Or, God didn't yet answer one of our prayers, so maybe He doesn't answer at all. When this happens, we lack outer and inner peace. Soon, we so busy ourselves that we become unable to rest.

Often the enemy tries to steal our hope as well. When we lose hope, we lose vision. As we lose vision, our interest and energy for the Kingdom work wanes. When this happens, we lose perspective of our own value in God and our sense of dignity. We consider ourselves to be damaged goods – similar to Moses, as he probably sat there thinking about how he was slow of speech and tongue. Next, we start to sear our conscience by believing lies. This makes us unable to take a stand against evil. Are we even able to distinguish between right and wrong at this stage? Rarely. Can we see the destructive goal Satan has in mind as he steals and robs from us?

The enemy tries to attack us as individuals, but obviously he attacks Christian projects, ministries and churches in the same way. He deflates courageous faith and attempts to steal our inheritance in Christ. He tries to paralyze our Christian workers with fear to the point where we seem unable to truly love Christ's body. Satan's goal is the church's total destruction.

Thankfully, Jesus doesn't stop with the warning about the robber coming to "steal, kill and destroy." He continues on in John 10:10, "*But* I have come that they might have life and have it more abundantly." How great is that? Where the enemy came to destroy, Jesus came to give life to the fullest! He wants to breathe life into our relationships, finances, families, character, love-life, friendships, governments, communities, nations and churches. In all the places where there is discouragement and despair – or other evidence of the enemy's theft – Jesus came to give us *life*. Ultimately, this means that there is hope for us as individuals as well as for our communities. Jesus can counteract all the enemy's doings as we listen to Him and obey His voice.

Specialists in building implosions use dynamite and a giant weight at the end of a crane to destroy buildings. In the same way, the enemy has effective tools for our destruction. One of his most significant ones is evident through how he uses *words*. Words are extremely powerful. It was by spoken words that our entire universe came into existence. That is the power of words when spoken by Almighty God. Our words, too, have power to create. James writes in chapter 3:9,10 of his book, that we have the power to bless and to curse with our words. He warns that our tongue can literally burn up our whole life (3:6). How many people have we seen whose entire careers have been torpedoed by something silly they said?

If I went up to a group of four-year-old children, pointed to a white board and then asked, "How many of you can draw?" kids would be fighting each other to get my attention.

Their hands would shoot up into the air and they would screech excitedly, "I can draw! I can draw! Pick me! Pick me!" Some would be standing there with their chests proudly sticking out and they would begin telling me about art they've drawn in the past. Yet, if I would go to that same group twenty years later to ask them the same question, the response would be very different. Most of them would look down at the ground, praying that I wouldn't pick them. Others would just stare at me or out a window. Maybe one person – the one who had had twenty years of art lessons – would slowly raise their hand and admit, "I can draw ... what kind of *drawing* did you mean?"

What happened between age four and age twenty-four?

Most likely, someone lied to them. Some authority figure, whether a teacher, parent or a relative, came along and saw their little four-year-old drawing and unkindly corrected them or degraded them. Maybe they said something like, "That's not how you draw a house. A house needs to have a window and a door with a handle. Your chimney is crooked. You don't get it. You can't draw. Here let me show you how to *really* draw."

The little four-year-old hears the criticism and believes the lie. When a spoken lie is believed, it becomes a curse in our life. Could it be that God may have created that little one with a gift of art? Maybe He had wanted that little child to communicate truth as an artist. As an adult now, it would literally take the resurrected Spirit of God in them to undo the damage.

The Bible tells us that our words have the power to bless people, bless churches, bless ministries, bless families, bless neighbors, bless nations or communities – or curse them. We can pronounce lies over people, or we can speak hope and encouragement.

We should not be quick to condemn fellow Christians or ministries. Are we blind to the curses we are pronouncing? We need to make a conscious effort *not* to go along with the work of our lying, stealing, murderous enemy. It's important to realize that when we accuse, we are participating with the accuser (Revelation 12:10).

I like to think in terms of our words being like a blade. When a murderer slashes his victim's flesh with a knife, it is violence. If a surgeon uses a knife to cut the flesh of his patients, it is healing. One knife is used for the purpose of killing, the other for the purpose of healing. Satan wants to destroy us with violent words, but God wants to heal us with His powerful Word. We, too, carry the knife in our hand – whether we destroy or heal is reflected from the motivation of our hearts.

So the enemy's motivation is rooted in fear and control, his goal is our destruction, and one of his most effective tools are words. Finally, there are four streams of shame that he often uses to drown us in condemnation.

The first stream is formed from something we've just mentioned: parents or authority figures who do not accept us as God made us to be. These are people who make us feel like we are never capable of measuring up to their expectations. We covered this in chapter one, when we talked about living in the shame zone. It's important for us to see that the enemy does all he can to reinforce negative feelings and emotions to destroy our hope, our vision or our pioneering spirit.

The second stream of shame is living in grace-less religion. Remember that fear and control leads us into religion, but love and freedom leads us into relationship. Grace-less religion is a judgmental system that is unable to extend forgiveness. This is not the *religion* mentioned in James 1:26,27, which might better be seen as *worship*. This is the kind of religion that cannot accept people at the various stages in their walk with God. It is critical, judgmental, and debasing. This kind of legalism stunts growth and can often come from people who have not truly accepted the grace of God into their own lives. They accept Jesus' forgiveness, but continue striving to work their way into pleasing God, mostly to "make up" for the junk of their past. Many of them have not heard of the importance of forgiving themselves.

I so desire for everyone to understand grace. Grace is God's enabling power. Although completely undeserved, God not only forgives, but He chooses to forget our sins and not hold them against us. That's not all! He awards us His restorative power to overcome and extends to us the opportunity for new beginnings.

The enemy uses a third stream to bring shame and condemnation into our lives: non-Biblical culture. Earlier, we mentioned the influence of Confucius in cultures and the ensuing result: women are seen as less valuable than men and so many girls grow up being ashamed that they are not boys. They just carry that shame around in their lives because of a culture that is not based on God's view of women.

If we read Proverbs 31, where it speaks of the woman of noble character, isn't it amazing what the Bible says about a woman's qualities and involvement? She is able work with her hands, bring in enough food for her family and the servants, interact in business as she buys a field and uses her earnings to plant a vineyard. She is strong and involved in profitable trading. She helps the poor and the needy, clothes her family according to the season, respects her husband, watches over the affairs of her household, speaks with wisdom and faithful instruction and receives praise at the city gate. Her husband also praises her, as do her children. This is one of the most honoring passages to women's design found in any piece of ancient literature; it is the Lord's view of women.

Another example of non-Biblical culture can be seen in our modern materialistic society. People are caught up in an unending rat race of owning a nicer home, a newer car, the most current gadgets, and a constantly changing wardrobe of stylish clothes. They are frantically buying the latest accessories and obsessing over a body that takes constant sculpting, all in an effort to be accepted by people who, at the end of our time on this world, won't matter. The enemy uses this kind of culture to make us continually dissatisfied. We read what Paul wrote in Philippians 4:11 and it almost seems impossible in our days, "I have learned to be content whatever the circumstances." Satan also uses this to bring condemnation to us when we have less than our neighbor. Maybe that's why the writer penned in Hebrews 13:5, "Keep your lives free from the love of money and be content with what you have, because God has said, 'Never will I leave you; never will I forsake you.'" Our contentment needs to be rooted in His presence, not in our materialism.

The fourth stream the enemy uses is abuse. It could be physical, emotional, verbal, sexual or spiritual abuse. To those who have been abused, let me reassure you that when your wound comes into the healing light of Jesus, the enemy completely loses his power. Don't be afraid to seek help to defeat the enemy's strategy.

Whatever the path, our enemy is trying to devour us. He uses words in an attempt to condemn us and these four streams of shame to open us up to his manipulation, lying, and robbery. He hopes that as we wallow in the position of victim, he can destroy the purposes of God in our friendships, marriages, families, communities, nations, and workplaces.

Of course, the fastest and healthiest way for us to experience healing from our enemy's attacks is through repentance and forgiveness. When we walk through those processes, we discover the full beauty of God's love and God's wonderful power of reconciliation.

## 14 | Repenting, Forgiving and Reconciling

It seems to me that many people who have experienced the enemy's attacks, feel their relationships in life are disjointed, fragmented and beyond repair. Girls have broken up with many boyfriends, ripping the core out of their ability to healthily relate or reconcile. Guys have done the same with girls. Parents have divorced, some multiple times; company loyalty is a phrase nobody understands; obedience has been relegated to the military and our minds have largely accepted the idea that although we are commanded by Jesus to love everyone, we don't have to like them.

Aren't you glad Jesus does not say to you, "I love you, but I don't like you?" or "I love you, but I just don't care to be around you?"

*Irreconcilable* differences in our relationships with people has really bothered me lately. I've always been of the opinion that people are mostly compatible – it's just a matter of what we're willing to give up, so others can be valued and treasured.

As I have pondered fragmented relationships and our apathetic complacency with brokenness, I've discovered that we need a greater understanding of the terms *repentance*, *apology* and *forgiveness*. As a matter of fact, it might surprise some people to consider that apologizing is not a Biblical concept at all.

Apologies are expressions of regret, remorse or sorrow for having insulted, failed, injured, or wronged a person or a group of people. It can also mean a defense or justification in speech or writing – which is where we get the concept of Christian Apologetics – a defense of our faith. Certainly, in reconciliation, defending or justifying our actions is not a healthy approach. Neither is "feeling bad" about something we have done, a way of reconciling. What is missing, is the most important component in forgiveness: taking responsibility and changing our minds, hearts and actions – the U-turn of walking away from the sin and towards God.

A friend of mine compared it to someone who gets pulled over for drinking and driving. By some miraculous intervention, the officer allows that man's sober friend to drive him home, but gives the drunkard a stiff fine. The second time that person gets pulled over for a DUI, he gets fined and put on probation. As soon as the probation is over, he does it again. This time he gets thirty days in jail, but when he's served his thirty days, he does it again.

Every time he gets caught he is very apologetic. He is sorry. He is crying. He is down on himself and so remorseful. In reality though, we can see that he is unrepentant. The only way to guarantee he does not get another DUI, is for him to never drink and drive again.

We are a society full of apologies with little repentance. What is the consequence? In this kind of society, there is not a change of heart and so there's very little rebuilding of relationships. Therefore, few people experience of the healing that comes with true repentance.

The flipside of the coin, of course, is forgiveness.

The first occurrence of the word forgiveness in the Bible appears in the story of Joseph and his brothers after their father Jacob has died. Joseph's brothers had sold him to some merchants, who sold him in Egypt. After Joseph's father dies, we read in Genesis 50:17 that his brothers are afraid and they approach their brother, saying, "Your father left these instructions before he died: 'This is what you are to say to Joseph: I ask you to forgive your brothers the sins and the wrongs they committed in treating you so badly.' Now please forgive the sins of the servants of the God of your father." And in the next verse, it goes on to read, "His brothers then came and threw themselves down before him. 'We are your slaves,' they said."

Right from the beginning, the word *forgive* in Scripture is accompanied with an idea we see throughout. Forgiveness is not just an apology, but it is accompanied with a willingness to sacrificially change – to pay back the debt. In this case, Joseph's brothers were willing to be his slaves! We can also call that accompanying action *repentance*.

Let's say, for example, a lady was gossiping about someone and then, moved by the conviction of the Holy Spirit, she goes to that person and apologizes for spreading vicious rumors. The victim reluctantly forgives her. I would suggest that the apology is not enough. What repentance would look like, in this specific case, is that she not only asked for forgiveness, but then went to all the people she had gossiped to and additionally ask them for forgiveness, setting the record straight each time. I'm sure that if she did that, the victim would not be forgiving reluctantly, but with great joy – not only because she apologized, but because she was being transformed by the power of humility.

David wrote in Psalm 130:4, "But with you there is forgiveness, so that we can, with reverence, serve you." It's not just an apology, but it includes service. We also see this reflected in the law – the Torah – when it comes to specific discipline for specific violations. In Exodus 22:7, for example, we read, "If anyone gives a neighbor silver or goods for safekeeping and they are stolen from the neighbor's house, the thief, if caught, must pay back double."

Knowing this, we can be inspired by Luke 19 and the story of Zacchaeus. He was a wealthy chief tax collector. When he interacted with Jesus, his response is noted in verse eight. "Zacchaeus stood up and said to the Lord, "Look, Lord! Here and now I give half of my possessions to the poor, and if I have cheated anybody out of anything, I will pay back four times the amount." And Jesus responds to him with, "Today salvation has come to this house …"

Zacchaeus was only required to pay back twice what he had stolen, but he volunteered to not only to pay back four times what he had stolen as a tax collector, but even to give half of his possessions to the poor. This action – this repayment – this transformation of the heart and its ensuing outward action is true repentance.

It seems that when we ask God for forgiveness for something we did, we are not repenting. Recently someone told me, "I feel like I keep asking God for forgiveness over and over for the same thing."

So I encouraged him and said, "Stop doing that and repent." Had he truly repented? Then, he would not be doing the same sin on a regular basis.

Repentance necessitates a complete change. A lifestyle change. An attitude change. A change of heart. A change of action. It is the accompanying idea to forgiveness. John the Baptist demanded of those who wanted to become his followers, "Produce fruit in keeping with repentance." (Luke 3:8)

The Bible defines forgiveness in 2 Corinthians 5:18-20 where we read, "All this is from God, who reconciled us to himself through Christ and gave us the ministry of reconciliation: that God was reconciling the world to himself in Christ, not counting people's sins against them." Simply, forgiveness is choosing to not hold someone's sins against them.

Forgiveness is not excusing, minimizing, justifying or tolerating the sin. It's not conditional on the other person's future behavior or an obligation to trust them. And it doesn't start with us feeling like forgiving. Forgiveness comes from a recognition that we are in need of healing and once we have recognized that need, it's simply a choice based on faith and obedience to God. We are trusting that His healing will come as we let go and move on – as we do for others as God has done for us. Really, it has almost nothing to do with the other person, but is a healing agent for our own relationship with God. As we move forward, we are able to be reconciled to Him which opens the door for reconciliation with the people around us. When that door opens, it's always amazing what God's Spirit is able to accomplish.

I remember my first speaking engagement in Japan like it was yesterday. I had gotten up onto the stage, stood behind the pulpit and got ready to deliver what I thought was a fairly good message. I was prepared to talk about why God created the nation of Japan and how His design for them was an important piece in the overall puzzle that makes up the nations of the world. However, before I could open my mouth and as I was looking at the congregation, I suddenly saw something that hadn't existed physically, but I knew was there. It was a wall. It was such a barrier for communication that I knew instantly that nothing I was about to say would be received by them.

"God?" I thought, as the Japanese translator stood beside me. "What is this wall?"

Very clearly, a non-contrived thought entered my head. "Derek, who are you?"

I was puzzled. "Is that a trick question, God? You just used my name and asked who I was?"

Apparently, God wasn't laughing. "Derek, who are you?"

I thought about the question. Obviously He meant more than my name. So, mentally I started off listing things in my identity. "I'm a man, I speak English as my primary language, I'm a pastor/teacher/speaker/writer, I'm Canadian, I live in Hawaii ..."

At that point I felt like someone had just slugged me in the stomach!

"Oh Lord, do you have a problem with Canadians?" I asked.

"Derek, what did Canada do to the Japanese in World War II?"

Good grief! I didn't know, really. I tried desperately to remember my Social Studies class in grade ten.

"We, um, we decided we couldn't trust the Japanese, so we herded them into camps until the war was over. Then we let them go. Do you mean *that*?"

"Derek, I gave Canada a beautiful gift – the gift of the Japanese people and their amazing attention to detail. You treated them horribly and it hurt them. It also hurt your nation. And it hurt and angered Me."

I was standing there embarrassed. Apparently God's perspective on my nation's history and my perspective were different.

"Derek?"

"Uh-huh?"

"Would you be willing to ask for forgiveness this morning – as a Canadian – of these Japanese people?"

"No!" I thought quickly. "Look, God. I wasn't even alive in WWII. That was a long time ago … and besides that, there are a lot of Canadians in this world – You could get someone more qualified to do this, if it's so important … and … I don't know … is this really You, God, or is it my own thinking? Maybe it's Satan! No … Satan wouldn't want me to ask for forgiveness." I sighed audibly. "It must be You, God."

Then, a verse popped into my head – it was from 2 Chronicles 7:14. "If my people, who are called by my name, will humble themselves and pray and seek my face and turn from their wicked ways, then I will hear from heaven, and I will forgive their sin and will heal their land."

Gently, God's Spirit encouraged me and convicted me all at the same time. "My son, you know how to pray – you're really good at praying. You know how to seek My face – it is one of the things I love about you. And you have turned from your wicked ways – that's great. Right now, however, you are ignoring the first phrase … if my people will humble themselves."

"Ah – h- h -." Guilty as charged. I was not big on humbling myself. As a matter of fact, I realized all of my responses were responses of pride. I didn't want to be associated with what Canada was guilty of. I wanted to be associated with my nation's greatness and beautiful future, not our sordid past. Yet, like wounded runners trying to run a race, it would indeed be better for us to get healed first.

"Okay, God."

By this time, although my Japanese translator was still smiling, she was wondering what on earth was going on. I started out slowly, "When I was introduced, it was said of me that I'm a Canadian living in Hawaii – and that is true. Knowing the histories of our nations, I think that before I get to my message I need to take some time to ask you, as Japanese people, for forgiveness." I went on to retrace the history as best as I could remember, then shared the perspective God had just given me, following it up sorrowfully, with, "It was wrong of us. It hurt both of our nations. It was especially hurtful to you, the Japanese people. So I am asking you now – will you please forgive me?"

I didn't know what to expect. I was hoping for fire from heaven. Nothing happened. Literally, *nothing happened*.

I stood there in silence.

Finally, I decided the wait was too excruciating. I would just go ahead and speak. Then, I strongly felt God saying, "*Wait.*"

So I waited. Waiting in front of a group of people with nothing but silence is very awkward. Had I passed the point of no return? I'd probably waited too long. In that case, I now had no more face to lose.

Maybe ten minutes later, a lady came, crying, down the aisle. She knelt in front of the stage and began to weep loudly. I went down and knelt beside her.

"I'm so sorry for what we did. Will you forgive us?"

"My family was directly affected," she explained between sobs. "When we got out of the camps, our house had been vandalized, our business had been destroyed, our car was stolen and our neighbors wouldn't talk to us."

I swallowed the lump in my throat. "How could we have been so stupid?" I was thinking.

"We decided we had to move back to Japan – so we did."

I knelt there, unsure of what to say. Finally she looked at me, deliberately speaking out the words, "I forgive you."

It was like a dam had broken. One by one, people came forward and spoke out their forgiveness to me.

In the midst of all this, a picture came to my mind. We were standing before the throne of God, each of us with something in our hands that was muddy, stinking, and even beyond recognition. God was taking it from us, washing it in the blood of Jesus and in water. Then, he was giving it back to us. It turned out we had been holding large, beautiful diamonds!

"Derek, these diamonds are your identities. All the tools I've given you to bring healing and restoration to people. The only question is, *how willing are you to humble yourself?*"

Our approach in the world needs to be in line with our calling to be ambassadors, as outlined in the context of the passage we've already looked at from 2 Corinthians 5:16-21:

> So from now on we regard no one from a worldly point of view. Though we once regarded Christ in this way, we do so no longer. Therefore, if anyone is in Christ, the new creation has come: The old has gone, the new is here! All this is from God, who reconciled us to himself through Christ and gave us the ministry of reconciliation: that God was reconciling the world to himself in Christ, not counting people's sins against them. And he has

committed to us the message of reconciliation. We
are therefore Christ's ambassadors, as though God
were making his appeal through us. We implore
you on Christ's behalf: Be reconciled to God. God
made him who had no sin to be sin for us, so that
in him we might become the righteousness of God.

When we get to the point where we do not "count
people's sins against them" any longer, we can move into a
spirit of love, humility and reconciliation. Do we love them
more than our fossilized opinion? Do we love others more
than ourselves?

Jacklyn was from Togo – in West Africa – and she was
staying with a Muslim family in Northern Africa. The father
of this family was known as being very radical. Had he known
that she was a Christian, there was a good possibility that her
life would have been in danger. One day, she made a colossal
mistake. She had finished her regular quiet time and had
opened the door to her room to go into the living room. At
that instant, the father walked by and saw her Bible lying on
her mat. She'd forgotten to hide it.

He grabbed her by the hair and threw her to the ground.
"I hate Christians! They are all a bunch of hypocrites," he
raved, his face dark with rage.

Jacklyn was afraid for her life and lay trembling at his
feet. She wanted to correct him and to put to use her training
in Christian Apologetics. She was going to say, "Well, Jesus is
not a hypocrite!" and go on to defend Christianity. Suddenly,
a deep grief welled up from within her heart – an
overwhelming sadness. "God," she asked, "What is this?"

"This is the grief on my heart for how Christians and
Muslims treat each other," was the immediate reply.

She looked up at the man's face and spoke, "It's true, what you say. It's true. There are many hypocrites in Christianity. We preach about loving our enemy, but we don't always act like it. And we have hurt Muslim people in many ways …" After speaking some more along those lines, she asked, "As a Christian, will you please forgive me?"

Tears welled up in his eyes. The rage in his face slowly dissolved. He walked away – unsure of how to respond, but he continued to allow Jacklyn to board there.

I was in Switzerland with some people who were praying about reconciliation in West Africa when Jacklyn recounted this story to us. "There was something really bizarre that happened when he walked away," she explained, "I'm almost hesitant to tell you because I don't want you to think I'm crazy."

We waited.

"When he walked away it was like I saw stuff falling from his ears … like the time in Acts 9:18 when scales fell from Saul's eyes – but this time it was from this man's ears."

As she said that, a passage of Scripture from John 18 came to mind. It recounts the drama surrounding the arrest of Jesus. We read, in verse ten, "Then Simon Peter, who had a sword, drew it and struck the high priest's servant, cutting off his right ear. (The servant's name was Malchus.)"

The sword, in Scripture, often represents the Word of God. Could there be nations and groups of people who can't hear what we're saying because we have been carelessly waving around Truth and cutting off their ears? Are we trying to reach people who can't hear what we're saying because of how wounded they are from us? Were this man's ears unplugged to hear about Jesus? Apparently so. Eight months later, he gave his life to Jesus and led his four wives and six children to do the same. The humility of Jacklyn had opened the door for this man to hear and respond to the Truth.

It is my strong desire that reconciliation, through forgiveness and repentance, be at the root of our approach to relationships – both as individuals and as concentric communities. In being Christians, our loving work for unity should be the most vibrantly colored thread in the tapestry of our lives and ministries.

## 15 | Moving Forward with Gratitude

At this point of the book, I hope you're already thinking about how you can share what you've learned with others. But, if you are hungering to be a part of something God wants to do in your generation and if you want to plant things of God into the lives of people around you, then you'll need to have the right heart attitude. Our personal mind-set is critical to any project's longevity. Many attempts to plant new things wither and die because they were started with a root of dissent, or grown with bitter and discouraged people. And most of *these* symptoms stem from ingratitude.

In Romans 1:24-31, we discover the tragic consequence of people who no longer want to give thanks to God. We read about how God gave these people over to the "lusts of their hearts to impurity and to the degrading of their bodies among themselves". Paul described how it led to all kinds of shameless sexual behavior, not only in the acts themselves, but in the consciences of the people who were ignoring God.

They no longer were ashamed of their loathsome conduct. So, God gave them over to a debased mind and they were filled with "every kind of wickedness, evil, covetousness, and malice." In his day, the Apostle saw them to be surfeited with envy, murder, strife, deceit, craftiness and much more. How did all that begin? The Bible says, "For though they knew God, they did not honor Him as God or give thanks to Him, but they became futile in their thinking, and their senseless minds were darkened." (Romans 1:21)

Isn't it amazing that ingratitude can lead to so much depravity? People just refused to acknowledge God and give Him thanks!

The very next verse shows us how this kind of ingratitude – and everything associated with it – multiplies. "They know God's decree that those who practice such things deserve to die—yet they not only do them but even applaud others who practice them." If we encourage people towards good, they will do more good. If we encourage others in their evil ways, they become more evil.

In Luke 17, we read about Jesus going into a village along the border between Samaria and Galilee. As He did, he was met by ten men with leprosy. They screamed out to Him, asking for His pity. When Jesus saw them, He said, "Go show yourselves to the priests." And we read in verse fourteen, that "as they went, they were cleansed." What an amazing miracle!

Here's a little side note. When someone prays over a person to be healed, it's okay for that person to go and get checked out by a doctor to confirm the healing. That's not a lack of faith – it's sensible. It's what Jesus did in sending them to the priests to be checked. Usually, God gets even more glory!

Then, we go on in the chapter and discover that when one of those ten lepers, a Samaritan, saw that he was "healed", he came back, praising God and throwing Himself at the feet of Jesus. Jesus wondered aloud why the other nine had not come back. Many a sermon has focused on how one of ten came to thank Jesus, encouraging us to be part of the minority in this instance! What has always puzzled me, was the last part of that passage. Jesus looks at the newly transformed man at his feet, and says, "Rise and go; your faith has made you well." What did Jesus mean? The others were healed, too. Did not their faith make them well? Why do we have three different English words for healing in this passage? Are we missing something that is clearer in the Greek New Testament? Yes, we are.

In English we read that as they went, they were cleansed and the Samaritan saw he was healed. After that, Jesus said the man's faith had made him well. These are not three synonyms for how his leprosy had miraculously disappeared. Instead, the first word, (*katharizo*, in Greek), refers to the kind of washing that removes dirt or stains from the skin. The second word (*iaomi*), speaks to being made whole – not just physically, but emotionally. Certainly anyone who had experienced healing from leprosy would find a peace they'd not known in a long while – a tranquility of spirit at being able to once again function as an accepted person in society.

The third word is the most exciting one! To the only one who came back and thanked Jesus, our Savior used the word *sozo* – the word for *saved* or *salvation*! This indicates that gratitude had opened the door for this leper to be saved. Isn't that fantastic? It reminds us of the thief hanging on the cross to whom Jesus granted an open door to paradise. The word also occurs in Matthew 1:21, where we read, "She will give birth to a son, and you are to give him the name Jesus, because he will *save* his people from their sins." In Acts 2:21b, we read, "… everyone who calls on the name of the Lord will be *saved*." Matthew 10:22, also includes that same word in the verse, "You will be hated by everyone because of me, but the one who stands firm to the end will be *saved*."

Jesus responded to a grateful Samaritan man, previously a leper, and rewarded him with salvation. That is the power of a thankful heart! If we contrast that with the passage in Romans 1, we come to understand that ingratitude is a spiral down to evil. Gratitude, on the other hand, opens the door for salvation. It isn't just a random statement of *I'm thankful*, but a happy heart of appreciation directed specifically to God, Himself.

Applying this account to our lives, we can think about all the people who have contributed to our understanding of God. Have we thanked them? I would encourage everyone to do so. Whether you are just working on rebuilding your own relationship with our loving Creator, or whether you're thinking about planting Him into the lives of the people around you and seeing what it is that He wants to grow, step forward with gratitude in your heart. God will bless those who are truly thankful with both the ability and the confidence they will need.

Having resolved to move with gratitude, we can be involved in what God is growing from the good seeds we have planted. I believe there is a coming a huge change in how we do and understand our calling as Christians. It may even revolutionize our approaches to what we know as church.

In the early 1950's, missionary work was largely considered to be a life-long calling to a nation far away, as it had been for centuries. When a person felt a call to go to Swaziland, for example, that person would plan to move there for the rest of their lives, often sacrificing ties to relatives, comforts of home and the education of their children in their motherland. Many wonderful missionaries made those kinds of long-term commitments. Their efforts continued to build on the groundwork that had been laid by generations before them, like the Jesuits who were sent to China in the 16th century. Then, in the decade of the 1950's, God launched ministries that used a new concept: short-term missions. At first, there was a lot of opposition by Christians in authority. But as time went on, many successful ministries such as the Billy Graham Crusades, Campus Crusade for Christ (now CRU), Operation Mobilization, Young Life, Youth With A Mission, the Southern Baptist Convention's Summer Missions Programs and many others were launched. They pointed out that short term missions was a Biblical idea – something we could see the disciples doing – going from village to village to share the good news of the Kingdom of God.

What was the reason for the paradigm shift at that time, in the way missions was approached? It all had to do with changes in technology.

In the year 1958, there were two giant leaps in the world of aviation. One was on October 4th, when the first transatlantic passenger jet service was launched from New York to London. Pan American started flights daily from New York to Paris on October 26th. The second big breakthrough came on December 10th of that same year, when National Airlines began to offer the first ever domestic flight – from New York to Miami. What this meant for missions, was that no longer did a new missionary have to take long, expensive ocean voyages, followed by tedious train rides, and maybe some horse or mule rides to get to where he or she had been called by God to go. Now, they could jump on a plane and fly there. By the 1970's and early 80's, short-term missions were in full swing and Christianity grew at a record pace. But, that record won't last long if we take hold of other technological changes that are sweeping our world, particularly the changes in communication technology.

The Great Commission has two primary verbs as themes, which we've mentioned already: *go* and *tell*. It's interesting that breakthroughs in transportation (going) and communication (telling) bring a surge in the growth of Christianity. Of course, it's not just Christianity that's on the move because of this, but ideas, in general, are now dispersing faster than ever before. What's exciting, is that we are witnessing the Holy Spirit coordinating moves of God, using technology, which previous generations had only dreamed of. Some Christians might think science and technology are not from God, but be assured, they actually originated from Him! After all, He is the author of all life and creativity.

The next great paradigm shift in missions is not only involving God's calling of missionaries to geographical regions, as He did when He called Hudson Taylor to China, but it will also include God's call into different areas of society – areas that cross geographical borders. What would happen, for instance, if Christians at a giant software company got together to pray, study the Bible, and strategize about how they could better love the people around them? What if Christians working for an influential media mogul would do the same? Or the Christians who work in a large factory? Or the Christian teachers in a public school? Or a group of godly professors in a state university? What would happen if Christians would stop seeing their jobs as just a means to a paycheck? Could all of us see ourselves as being where God planted us in order to firmly plant what we know of Him into the lives of other people? Thinking through what church could look like in the midst of this shift, is an important focus that we all need to think about.

Certainly, if we would yield our minds to these ideas, God would use an open door to pour out His Spirit on His children. In Joel 2 we read that the nation allowed wickedness to spread "like blackness upon the mountains" and Joel writes about how horrible everything got. Before that evil time, the people were in "anguish" and their faces "grew pale." God urges them, pleads with them really, to "return to me with all your heart, with fasting, with weeping, and with mourning." Were that to happen, Joel said, the Lord would not allow the nation to collapse, but would move swiftly to protect and bless it. We read in verse twenty-five, "I will repay you for the years that the swarming locust has eaten, the hopper, the destroyer, and the cutter, my great army, which I sent against you." Then, in verse 28, we read, "Afterward, I will pour out my Spirit on all flesh; your sons and your daughters shall prophesy, your old men shall dream dreams, and your young men shall see visions."

My purpose in writing this book was two-fold: to plant what I've learned about God into your life and to have you plant it into someone else's life. God wants us to know Him in a deep, personal, life-changing way. But almost as significantly, God wants us to plant Him into the lives of those around us. This is how He is able to move in our communities ... through people like you. Let's not be people who say *come and listen*, let's be people who gratefully *go and tell*. Then, we get to be a part of what He wants to grow.

If you would like to download a free study guide to use for further individual reflection or a group book study, you can download *Planting God, The Study Guide* from www.facebook.com/plantinggod.